I LEARNED MORE THAN THEM; TRUE STORY

ABOUT MIDDLE SCHOOL STUDENTS EDUCATING A TEACHER

BILL MASSEY

I never liked being called an educator. No one ever says, "When I grow up, I want to be a physician." The same holds true for aspiring teachers.

— BILL MASSEY

TOPICS AND TIDBITS

STUDENT FOREWORD

In 2005, I went into my elective art class thinking I was going to have so much fun. After the first day, I realized it was going to be an art history class too, and that my teacher, Mr. Massey, didn't play. I skipped class a lot, and barely passed with a *D*. But me almost failing his art class as a seventh grader did not stop Mr. Massey from selecting me in eighth grade to be in his AVID (Advancement Via Individual Determination) class—a pilot program for Granville County Schools focused on preparing students for high school, and ultimately for college. I was not happy about that, and made it known to my mom.

"AVID class, in addition to all my other school work, is going to be too much for me," I complained. But my mom made it known in no uncertain terms that if she, as a single parent of a teenager, could work two jobs while completing her master's program, then me completing eighth grade, including AVID class, was not going to be a big deal, for either of us.

After the first week of AVID class, which included a year-beginning parent/teacher conference night and a lengthy conversation between my mom and Mr. Massey, in my presence, I decided it best that I get my act together, quickly. I did not want my mom coming up to school again and have to "show herself," as she put it.

Inspired by and respectful of my mom's challenges, I undertook the responsibilities of my core academic classes—math, language arts, science, social studies—as part of the AIG (Academically and Intellectual Gifted) program, was the student manager for my middle school's football team, tutored some of the players, wound up becoming a pretty good artist in Mr. Massey's art class, including having some of my work exhibited in our school's art gallery, and, was one of the top students in Mr. Massey's AVID class.

I was also captain of my AVID class, responsible for making sure the academic notebook—a big-deal requirement of the program—of every student was up-to-date and in order, and that all homework was completed and submitted. This required no-exceptions, no-excuses maintenance of our AVID notebooks, taught us all how to organize, prioritize, create daily and weekly agendas, and how to study and prepare for tests. Funny thing is, that was twelve years ago, and I still have my notebook. I even refer to it from time to time.

In addition to fairly but firmly holding our feet to the fire academically, Mr. Massey also made sure his students stood out in the crowd by encouraging us to dress for success.

Some of my most vivid memories of Mr. Massey are of how he respected his students and their parents. For instance, on my first report card in eighth grade, I made my first and only D ever—in science, one of my favorite subjects, of all things. When some of my teachers questioned my mom's commitment to my education because she missed that particular parent/teacher conference, Mr. Massey came into the room and explained to my other teachers that my mom was unwavering in her support of me, but as a town commissioner, she had to attend a conflicting commissioners' meeting that night. In doing that, Mr. Massey created a newfound level of respect for my mom among my teachers, and a newfound appreciation within me for parents like my mom, who support their children, and their teachers— support that can change a child's future. My mother did that for me.

After I got that *D*, Mr. Massey, aware that while my mom was thoroughly disappointed in that grade, she was also working full time while finishing up her master's degree thesis, started closely monitoring my progress in science class, and every Friday he had me take a progress reports home to be signed by my mom and returned to him on Monday. Not many teachers would do that. That was not his subject. But I was his student.

There were few dull moments in AVID class. Mr. Massey constantly found ways to make learning exciting. Fun. But I knew better than to test the dedication of Mr. Massey or my mom to my education. They were determined. And that determination instilled in me the courage and confidence to undertake many extracurricular activities, in addition to academics.

Mr. Massey was a tough teacher, with high expectations and old-school beliefs. He loved his students and thoroughly enjoyed teaching us life-skills. But most importantly, he wanted us all to know that to get respect, you must give respect. "A nice person will go much farther in life than a smart grouch," he told us. That is something I value to this day.

At the end of my eighth-grade year, I received an award for "Most Improved Student," because I had a mom and a teacher who cared and recognized in me something special.

As an adult, I stay in touch with Mr. Massey. His kind toughness opened my mind to the importance of leadership skills, and in using them to help others achieve their goals.

Mr. Massey—thank you for not giving up on me after that first day in seventh grade, when I almost gave up on myself. And thank you for being an empowering teacher. Your class positively impacted me on so many levels.

Oh, by the way, I still have every congratulatory postcard and birthday card you sent me, and every update letter you sent to my mom over the years!

Phylicia Barker, student, 2005 – 2007

PARENT FOREWORD

My daughter and I have both completed seven years of education, without any major issues with teachers. All Phylicia's teachers loved her in elementary school. But eighth grade started off a bit bumpy. Phylicia complained about her teachers, for the first time, ever. I received notes from teachers about failing grades, for the first time, ever. That was not my child! Someone or something had abducted my daughter and left a stranger.

"Phylicia, what is going on with you and school?" I asked.

"Being in AVID class, in addition to all the eighth-grade schoolwork, is too much for me," she said, not knowing how I would react.

"Phylicia, the only thing you have to do is go to school and behave. That is your job. I am working two jobs, completing and graduating from a master's program, running a household, and being a single parent to a teenage daughter. THAT is what you might call TOO MUCH," I said, with a tone that made Phylicia take a step back.

The first week of school, I attended parent/teacher orientation at Phylicia's middle school, primarily intent upon speaking with her art and AVID teacher. When we walked into his classroom, student artwork on the walls caught my eye. While waiting for our turn, Phylicia began explaining to me the meaning of each detail in each piece of art; her way of trying to get me on her side, before we spoke with her teacher about her disenchantment with his class. I know my child.

Soon, a tall man walked over, introduced himself, and politely invited us to take a seat. Phylicia immediately began making her case by stating her so-called reasons for needing to get out of AVID class.

"Momma, I can't do all the work Mr. Massey requires in AVID, in addition to my other five classes, and be equipment manager for the football team, too," she pleaded, hoping I had changed my mind from our discussion a couple of days earlier.

Mr. Massey waited and listened patiently as I explained priorities to my daughter and laid out the differences between what she wanted to do versus my requirements for what she had to do as long as she lived under my roof.

When the conversation ended, after Phylicia stopped crying, she found herself still enrolled in AVID class—a decision that would ultimately result in her becoming much more productive in all her classes. It didn't happen overnight; it was a process. Phylicia even made a D in science that first quarter. But ultimately it helped her achieve and maintain an A/B grade average. And it helped put an end to the negative notes and telephone calls I had been receiving about Phylicia's attitude and behavior.

Mr. Massey made a great deal of impact upon Phylicia's education and life. She began showing leadership abilities and taking on more responsibilities. I saw my child begin growing into a young woman.

Currently, Phylicia is enrolled in Wake Technical Community College majoring in Construction Technology Management, working for a district court judge, waitressing at a coffee shop, modeling, and starting her own fashion magazine. I am convinced being in AVID class and encountering Mr. Massey, encouraged Phylicia's confidence and maturity to levels she never imagined.

Thank you, Mr. Massey, for your kindness, love of learning, and sharing it with others. Old-school teachers are the best!

Tonya Sneed, parent

HOW I GOT MYSELF INTO THIS

For the better and worst parts of three decades, I held various positions in sales, marketing, and/or advertising for a variety of companies. One had five employees. Some were Fortune Top 5. I was being paid quite well, but I was burned-out, and I knew it. But I would have continued to plug along in that velvet rut, save for an early January 2003 business lunch conversation with Sarah, a sales rep for one of my ad agency's printing vendors.

"What else would you do, if you could do whatever?" Sarah casually asked while pouring thousand island dressing on her salad, after I had expressed discontent with my now less-than-fulfilling job.

"Teach," I immediately replied.

"Teach what, marketing, at a college?"

"No. Teach kids. About art."

"My daughter-in-law, Beth, is principal of a middle school,

one county over, but it's only a twenty-minute drive. Want me to set you up to talk to her?"

Sarah did that, and I met with Beth a week later, and Beth referred me to another principal at another middle school in her district.

"Mr. Callaghan has an opening for an art teacher, right now. Want me to arrange for you to meet with him?"

Beth did that too, and within two weeks I had interviewed with Dan, interviewed with an assistant superintendent, interviewed with the superintendent, and was back in Dan's office for a follow-up interview.

"Before we pursue this further, I think it only fair that you talk to another of my teachers who left his former life to do this job; he has been here since the beginning of this year," Mr. Callaghan said. "He is in his planning period, right now, so come with me," he instructed.

We walked down a long hallway and around a corner to a large classroom on the main corridor, where Mr. Callaghan introduced me to Boyce Harvey, and left us to it.

"Let's walk over to the media center, where it's quieter and more comfortable," Mr. Harvey said.

We talked for about thirty minutes. He was honest, but encouraging and supportive. Turned out, he got into teaching by retiring from the federal government, so he could hold his son Brian's teaching position for him, after Brian was called to active duty and deployment to Iraq with his NC National Guard unit.

Note: *When Brian returned from Iraq a year later, he took advantage of an opportunity to teach at the high school, which worked out well, because Boyce wanted to continue teaching.*

"The position teaching art here is yours, if you still want it," Mr. Callaghan said, when he and I got back together after my chat with Mr. Harvey.

"I do," I said.

"Be forewarned; it's the hardest job you'll ever have."

"Oh, I don't know about that. I mean, I did grow up on a cotton farm. And I was in Vietnam, twice."

"Different kind of hard," Mr. Callaghan said.

"So, I'll start next school year, huh?"

"No. I haven't had an art teacher for these kids in more then three months; it's hard to find someone who wants to teach way out here in the boonies," he explained. "We just started second semester. So, I need you to start right away."

"How about I start at the end of the month?"

"How about you start next week?"

We settled on me starting in two weeks. I had never done anything that impulsive in my life. But, buoyed by their candor and obvious dedication and sincerity, I was totally at ease trusting Mr. Callaghan and Mr. Harvey, right off the bat.

When I started teaching, there was an acute teacher shortage in North Carolina, especially in outlying rural, economically repressed counties. While my degree in art and design with a minor in art history qualified me to teach eleven- to fourteen-year-olds, I wasn't licensed, as required by law, in public schools. So I—like Mr. Harvey—entered the profession under the Lateral Entry Program, a program that allowed college graduates who were *qualified* by professional experience, to start teaching a related subject, in conjunction with becoming *certified* in that subject.

There is a special place in heaven for all teachers, but

lateral entry teachers should be near the top of the list. We were allowed two years to complete four to six requisite college classes, then pass the North Carolina teacher certification exam—unaffectionately known as the *Praxis.* That process involved teaching six classes by day while preparing lesson plans and grading papers by night, simultaneous with taking education-related college courses whenever and wherever available. In my particular case, I attended classes at four different local universities on Tuesday and Thursday evenings and on Saturday mornings, until I completed my six prescribed courses. That was a grind, but, as Rocky Balboa so eloquently put it, "A man's gotta do what a man's gotta do, ya know?"

2

BEST LAID PLANS

"I'll have Miss Adcock, an experienced teacher and lateral entry mentor, in your classroom with you for your first week," Mr. Callaghan promised the day I accepted the job.

Whew!

I immediately set about closing out my ad agency responsibilities and preparing for my teaching career. I purchased, read, and practically memorized *First Days of School*—the new teacher's Bible—written by Dr. Harry Wong. Accordingly, at Dr. Wong's behest, I prepared ten days of lesson plans—"Better to plan too much than plan too little," he had noted—and prepared photocopy-handouts of *The Five Ps of Classroom Expectations:*

Be Prompt

Be Present

Be Prepared

Be Participatory

Be Polite

In middle school parlance, that translates to mean:

Beat the tardy bell

Don't skip by hiding out in the bathroom

At the very least, bring a pencil to class

Don't mumble, "I don't know," when asked a question

Behave yourself

"Middle school students don't like the word *Rules*, so call them *Expectations*," Dr. Wong advocated.

I was ready.

"Miss Adcock has to fill-in for another teacher who is unexpectedly ill and will be out for a while, so you'll be on your own," Mr. Callaghan said, the first day I showed up for work.

I was not *that* ready.

I steeled myself for the challenge ahead by telling myself that, "I am probably smarter than most of them, and surely bigger than any of them." (As it turned out, that last part was not true. Ricky, one of my eighth graders, was the size of an NFL linebacker.)

3

DAY ONE: PART ONE

Bright and early on a crisp, cold Monday morning, I reported for my first day as a public school teacher. Mr. Callaghan spent about five minutes with me—two of which he was on the phone with a disgruntled parent whose child had missed the school bus—before he scurried away to monitor the arrival of buses delivering kids who had *not* missed their busses. That left me to find my way to my new classroom on my own.

I roamed the main corridor until, with minimal directions from a custodian—Mr. Wilkerson, according to the name patch sewn to his shirt—I located Room 219 ... about as far from the front office as it could possibly be.

When I entered my classroom, it appeared to have been last vacated by a stampeding herd of wild buffalo. Tables were skewed, chairs were scattered, and trash was strewn.

At 7:15 a.m., the first bell rang, and my seventh-grade

homeroom students began trickling in. According to my class roster there would be twenty-eight of them. Per Dr. Wong's suggestion, I met them at the door and greeted them welcomingly. Some grunted back. Some rolled their eyes. Most ignored me.

At 7:18, the tardy bell rang. Only twenty students were present. A minute later, five of the delinquents—all girls—strolled in, gossiping and giggling. A couple of minutes after them, the final three boys graced me with their presence.

So much for *P Number 1—Be Prompt.*

By that time, a sizeable group of girls had congregated around one table in a far corner and were noisily polishing nails or applying make-up. Another group of six boys had taken seats at a back-of-the-room table and commenced a poker game, replete with one-dollar bills. A couple of girls were sashaying around the room, table-to-table, spiritedly socializing with anyone willing to participate. And two boys had their heads down and were already sound asleep.

"Please take your regular seats, so I can take roll," I requested over the din of laughter and chatter, in my most teacher-like voice. A few kids deigned to look over at me as though I were a Martian, but most assumed I was just another authority-less sub, I suppose, and did not bother to budge. Louder than the first time, I said again, "Please take your seats." That time, everyone ignored me. "Wonder what Harry Wong would do, at this moment?" I pondered.

I walked slowly over to the large, heavy, oak wood classroom door ... and slammed it shut as hard as I could. The walls shook. There was a loud chorus of startle-born shrieks. Then the room fell dead silent. No one ignored me then. The kids stared at me with saucer-sized eyes. I stared back. There was a knock on the door. It was the music teacher, Mr. Peters, from the classroom next door.

"Everything okay over here?" he inquired, gazing past me at the kids.

"It is now," I replied.

"Good morning. I am Mr. Massey, your new, permanent, full-time teacher; there will be no more subs," I said, addressing the class after walking to the front of the room. The kids looked around at each other, then back at me. "Now ... please get in your regular seats ... so I can take roll," I said, with deliberate determination.

"We don't have assigned seats. We sit anywhere we want," one student—Courtney, as it turned out—brazenly informed me.

"Well, you'll have assigned seats soon. But for now, sit anywhere. But sit."

The first thing I did after taking roll was distribute what I called "My Cardinal Rule" handout.

"What's that?" someone in the middle of the pack snidely asked, before they even had a copy of whatever *that* was. I ignored her.

"These are my two promises to you; to all of you," I said, once everyone had a copy in hand. I waited a long moment for them to read it, or at least glance at it.

"Promise number one: You will not be bullied in our class, by anyone," I read, loudly, then waited for it to sink in a bit. I had heard and read enough about it to know that mean-spirited bullying was dangerously rampant among middle-schoolers. "Promise number two: You ... will not ... bully anyone ... in our class," I continued without referring to the sheet. I wanted them to know I meant it. At the bottom of the page was my signature; not quite John Hancock big, but big, and official looking.

I repeated those promises to all my students in all my classes that day.

At 7:38, the homeroom dismissal bell rang. The kids shot out of their chairs as though fired from a cannon and stormed the door, where I had taken up station to bid them a good school day.

"Go back to your seats, please, until I dismiss you," I said, realizing I should have anticipated that. They stopped and stared. I stared back and calmly waited.

"The bell dismisses us," someone in the mob snapped. It was Courtney. Again.

"No, the bell tells me it's time for *me* to dismiss you ... properly. And stampeding out of here as if the room is on fire, leaving it in a shambles for the next class, is not proper. Now, please take your seats, and let's try this again."

There was a lot of grumbling, and a smattering of mumbled profanity, but order prevailed. By that time, my first-period class of sixth-grade art students was noisily congregating in the doorway, observing the spectacle.

I turned to them and said, "Please line up along the wall, out of the doorway, so these ladies and gentlemen can exit the room, when I dismiss them."

I turned my attention back to my homeroom kids.

"When I ask you to do so ..." I began, but as soon as I uttered the first word, a half-dozen kids bounded out of their seats. I stopped talking and waited. One by one they resentfully sat back down. "When I ask you to do so, please stand, slide your chair under the table, and depart the room properly. No running."

"We're going to be late to first period," Courtney griped.

"We'll do better tomorrow, I'm quite certain. Won't we?" I replied.

Courtney seemed to be the de facto homeroom spokesperson, so after that first day, I had her call roll each morning. She seemed to relish the responsibility. Besides, I couldn't pronounce half their names correctly.

DAY ONE: PART TWO

MY HOMEROOM PERIOD WAS FOLLOWED BY SIX 45-MINUTE ART classes—two classes each of sixth, seventh, and eighth graders, twenty-eight to thirty-two students per class—with a lunch period in between, and a planning period at the end of the school day. Every one of those first-day art classes was basically a repeat of my homeroom experience. By day's end, I knew how Bill Murray must have felt in the movie *Groundhog Day*. Those art classes had also been monitored by unlicensed subs for the previous thirteen weeks; subs who had allowed my students to pretty much rule the roost and do whatever they pleased.

"So what? It's only art; we won't gonna learn anything, anyway," Denise, one of my fifth-period eighth graders said in her attempt to explain why that situation had been acceptable. That's when it became obvious that Denise, like Courtney, had appointed herself class mouthpiece. There was one in each period.

"What did you learn today that is going to help you tomorrow?" my wife Gerry asked when I got home from the longest workday of my professional life.

"Two things: That middle schoolers are like those little Whack-A-Moles; when their teachers sit down, they start popping up."

"And the second thing?"

"That chewing gum in class is life sustaining for them, like breathing. One of the first questions pleadingly asked in every class, was, 'Can we chew gum in here?'"

"And you said?"

"I figured, why fight a meaningless battle? So, I said, 'I don't know if you can chew gum in here or not; I've never seen you try. But, if you can, you may. But you need to know two things: First, if I see bubbles being blown, or hear gross smacking of gum, the offenders will have to spit their gum into the wastebasket. And secondly, if I find one piece of gum stuck under a chair or a table, gum-chewing privileges will cease for everyone ... for a month.'"

"But there's already a bunch of gum stuck under there ... and I didn't do it," someone quickly pointed out.

"Me either," I said, firmly.

"Me either," someone else declared, igniting a chorus of other denunciations.

"Tomorrow, I'm bringing in a couple of putty knives. Homeroom and each art class will use them to remove all the gum stuck under one randomly chosen table and the four chairs at that table. That'll take care of seven of our eight tables," I explained. "And, just to be fair, I'll do the last table myself, even though 'I didn't do it either,'" I said.

By the end of the week, despite abundant exclamations of "Ooos" ... "Yuck" ... and "Gross" ... all tables and chairs had been de-gummed.

That weekend I went to Walmart and bought the biggest bag of Bazooka bubble gum I could find, to be dispensed as rewards for uncommon valor in class.

"Remember what I said about finding gum stuck somewhere it ought not be," I told each class on Monday morning, as I passed the bag of gum around.

"Can I have two pieces?" someone in one of the classes asked.

"Sure ... if a classmate is willing to give you his or hers," I replied. There were no takers.

5

DAY TWO: DÉJÀ VU

ON MY SECOND DAY, WHEN THE TARDY BELL RANG FOR homeroom, I closed the classroom door. The same eight kids who were tardy the day before, again arrived late to class, but discovered the door was locked. They knocked. I ignored them. They banged. I still ignored them. At some point later, our assistant principal, Mrs. Thomas, came across them sitting on the hallway floor, outside our classroom. She unlocked the door, stepped inside, and motioned me over. She and I had a brief discussion, in front of the repeat offenders, about my expectation that everyone be prompt to class.

"I had that same conversation with these same ladies and gentlemen when they were tardy yesterday," I explained.

Mrs. Thomas departed with the eight ne'er-do-wells in tow. I went back inside and switched them from tardy to absent in my roll book.

My first-period class had four locked-door late arrivers

and my second-period class had three. All were eventually swept up by Mrs. Thomas and whisked away to the front office. None of my after-lunch classes had any delinquencies. "Word had gotten around that there's a new sheriff in town, and he don't play," Mrs. Thomas later pointed out.

On day three, my third-period class of seventh graders took strenuous exception to my insistence upon everyday punctuality.

"We can't get here ... all the way from B-Hall ... in three minutes. It's all the way on the other side of the building," they protested.

My reply, "This isn't the Pentagon," was met with "Huh"-like blank stares.

"Meghan, go to the gym and ask Coach Kozak if I can please borrow a stopwatch for a few minutes. Bring it over to B-Hall." Meghan stared at me. "Go on, hustle, but don't run in the hallway," I told her. "The rest of you, please line up at the door."

Meghan took off toward the gym, and the rest of us marched over to B-Hall. In short order, Meghan returned and handed me the stopwatch.

"Now, all of you go back to our classroom and get in your seats. Don't be noisy, and don't run, but don't lollygag, either."

They headed back down the corridor. I started the watch and followed. When everyone was back in our room and seated, I stopped the watch and glanced at it.

"So how long do you think that took?" I asked. No one spoke. "Come on, take a guess."

"Longer than three minutes, that's for sure," Cory replied.

"Cory, come up here, look at the watch, and tell us how long that took," I said.

"I can't read no stopwatch," he grumped back.

"I can," Tiana said. I held out the watch. She came up and took it. "Two minutes ... and ... ten, eleven, twelve ... two minutes and twelve seconds," Tiana proudly announced, then returned to her seat.

"So, how much time did you have to spare?" I asked. Again, no one spoke for a long moment, until Tiana sheepishly raised her hand. I acknowledged her.

"Forty-eight seconds."

"Ta da."

Thereafter, instances of tardiness were few and far between; with one notable exception. Several weeks later, five of my students showed up ten minutes late to third-period class. They tapped on the classroom door. I answered and gave them my what-can-I-do-for-you look. No one spoke.

"Where have you been?" I finally asked.

"Miss Cash held us back to finish our language arts assignment," one of them said.

"Do you have a note from Miss Cash, saying that?" No response. "Then go back and get one."

"All of us?"

"You're all late, aren't you?"

The following week, the same five kids were tardy again, that time by fifteen minutes. They tapped on the door. When I answered, Tameisha held out a scrap of paper.

"What's that?"

"A note from Miss Cash."

"Go back, all of you, and tell Miss Cash I said you can

spend the rest of this class period with her; that my class has already started, and we're in the midst of an assignment," I said, without taking the note from Tameisha.

That afternoon, as soon as teachers were dismissed from departure bus duty, I went back to my classroom and began washing the table work surfaces with Pine-Sol. Within minutes, Miss Cash marched in, followed closely by Mrs. Thomas, and assailed me with her version of how "an experienced teacher" would have "dealt with" the set-to between she and I from earlier in the day.

"Listen, here's how I handle things when students are late to my class: I will always—" she started to say. I held up my hand to stop her. Ordering me to "listen," irked me.

"You may handle tardiness to your classes any way you see fit, I don't care," I said, with undue respect. Miss Cash drew back. Mrs. Thomas tensed up.

"What?" Miss Cash asked, aghast.

"You handle tardiness your way, I'll handle it mine."

"Uh ... uh ... well," Miss Cash exclaimed, whirled, and stormed out of my classroom. Mrs. Thomas looked at me, shook her head, threw up her hands, and followed. I went back to killing germs.

Early the next morning, long before school was scheduled to start, Mrs. Thomas walked into the admin support area where I was making copies. She tried not to grin, but had to, just as I tried not laugh, but...

"I told Miss Cash storming down to your classroom was not a good idea, not in her state of mind, but she insisted. All I could think to do was tag along, as a referee," Mrs. Thomas told me. "The whole time you two were verbally locking horns, I was thinking, 'Surely in my million hours of administrator training, they must have said something about how to diffuse a situation like that,' but I couldn't for the life of me remember what."

Students from Miss Cash's class were never again tardy to my class, not on her account, and Miss Cash and I became fairly good friends. In fact, Miss Cash was famous for her legendary homemade sausage & cheese balls, and every time she made some, she brought me a dozen or so, making our truce well worth it, to me.

6

AYE AYE, CAPTAIN

AFTER I GOT A FEEL FOR THE INDIVIDUAL NATURE OF MY students in each of my classes, usually about two weeks in, I appointed class captains. Most often, I chose the most rambunctious kid in each class. I figured, since they wanted to be jumping up and scurrying around the room anyway, why not harness their hyperactivity, and put it to good use passing out supplies, taking up quiz papers, returning graded quizzes, collecting completed art projects, and the like. I also had a two-birds-one-stone ulterior motive for

selecting the most ants-in-the-pants students as captains —keeping them near me. "You can't assist me from the back of the classroom. I need you seated up here, close to my desk," I would explain.

Sometimes my first choices worked out, but sometimes, not so much. In those instances, I did not hesitate to switch horses in mid-stream. Even in mid-class, if need be.

On the first day of the second, third, and fourth quarters, I selected new class captains. Occasionally, a previous class captain who had been relieved of duty for ill behavior would be given a second chance, if he or she had earned it. And occasionally, a student who had been deposed as class captain the previous year, say as a sixth grader, would be given a second chance when he or she reached seventh or eighth grade.

7

PAINT BY NUMBERS

MY FIRST WEEK AS A TEACHER, I GAVE THE KIDS THE BENEFIT OF the doubt, trusting they could sit at a table with their friends without being disruptive. My bad. They could not. So, that Saturday, I went into school and spray-painted the surfaces of the eight classroom student worktables a different color—red, yellow, blue, purple, green, orange, black, or white. On Sunday afternoon, the paint having had sufficient time to dry, I went back and, using a black, broad felt-tip permanent Magic Marker, hand wrote a seat number—1, 2, 3, and 4—on the corners of every table. On the black table, I used a small paintbrush and white model airplane paint.

When the kids reported to class on Monday, I met them in the hallway, just outside the classroom door.

"There are seven lists posted on the wall beside the door. One is for homeroom. The others are for art class periods, one through six," I informed them. "Please line up along the wall, out of the hallway, then, one at a time, check the list for your name, find your assigned table color and seat number, then go in and have a seat at that table, in that seat." There was an immediate undercurrent of moaning and groaning.

"Where's the purple table at?" homeroom student Desiree grumped, after checking the list.

"Well it ain't out here in the hall, girlfriend," her joined-at-the-hip friend Keisha replied. Desiree smacked her lips and stormed into the room. After all the kids were inside, I walked in and looked at Desiree, sitting in her assigned seat, her arms folded in defiance. Keisha's assigned seat was all the way across the room. I smiled. They did not.

In every class, kids whose assigned seats were quite intentionally separated from their friends were not happy. Neither was our custodian, Mr. Hunt, when he came in during my lunch period to empty our wastebaskets, only to discover that, despite my best efforts not to, I had gotten a fine multi-colored mist of spray paint on the light beige linoleum floor he had waxed and buffed the previous Friday afternoon, after school.

Several colleagues had warned me that being on the outs with our custodians was not a good thing. "Especially when a student pukes in your classroom," one of them said. "If you've been respectful of them, they'll clean it up right away. If you haven't, they'll leave you with a mop and a water bucket with that squeegee attachment thing on the side, and let you fend for yourself."

I stayed late that afternoon and helped Mr. Hunt buff out my floors. And I never had to clean up any puke.

8

MY KINGDOM FOR A PENCIL

ALMOST FROM DAY ONE OF MY TEACHING CAREER, I STARTED every class period with a one-question quiz that had no possible wrong answers. "If you could be famous as a painter, or famous as a sculptor, which would you rather be famous for, and why?" is an example of a typical question. I did that for two reasons: one, to settle the kids down as quickly as possible, and two, to get them to start thinking critically. "You never know how you really feel about something until you write about it; writing makes you think," I told the kids. Problem was, right from the get-go, someone in every class would woefully declare, "I don't have a pencil to take the quiz with," which would immediately be followed by, "Me neither" … "Me neither" … "Me neither."

At the beginning of my second week, I gave each of my 162 students two brand new, already sharpened, Ticonderoga #2 pencils.

"These are real wood; the good kind," Mariah gleefully proclaimed when she got hers. The kids who had pencils usually had the fake-wood, ten-for-a-dollar, "Back to School Special" Walmart kind; the kind you could not sharpen to a useable point if your life depended upon it.

"I'll give each of you two new pencils on the first day of each quarter," I promised. "But that's it. If you lose them, or break them, or forget to bring them to class, don't ask me for another one; borrow one from a classmate," I said. "However, if you use it up, bring the worn-down nub to me, and I'll give you a new one."

"What about if I wear-out my erasers?" Mariah asked.

The next day, as I greeted the kids at the door, when Mariah arrived at class I quietly slipped a big, Pink Pearl eraser into her hand. She grinned ear to ear.

By the way: The answer to the one-question quiz example cited above, about

being a painter or a sculptor, was almost always, "I'd rather be a famous painter," and the number one reason as to why was, "Sculpting is too much work."

Despite my benevolent efforts, almost immediately kids were showing up to class without their newly acquired pencils, or any pencil for that matter.

"Mr. Massey, do you have a pencil?" Kenny asked, about three days after I had handed out free pencils.

"Yes. I do. But thank you for asking," I replied, and kept checking attendance. Some kids got it, but most were bewildered by my reply.

"I meant, I don't have one," Kenny clarified.

"Bummer," is all I said as I flipped my roll book shut. That became my standard refrain to declarations of unpreparedness.

"I don't have any notebook paper."

"Bummer."

"I didn't do my homework."

"Bummer."

"I forgot to get my permission slip signed."

"Bummer."

"I left my backpack in Mr. or Mrs. So-and-So's classroom."

"Bummer."

One day, as the kids in my fourth-period class of seventh graders were rustling notebook paper in preparation for that day's one-question quiz, someone behind me too loudly whispered to someone else, "I don't have a pencil."

"Bummer," Cynthia, one of my students from the Masonic Home for Children, immediately replied, not even pretending to whisper.

There were lots of snickers. I smiled at her mimicry.

"I don't have no notebook paper, neither," the pencil-less person added.

"Double bummer," Cynthia said.

From that day forth, whenever a fourth-period student acknowledged being unprepared, I would look over at Cynthia, and she would calmly say, "Bum...mer." She came to take great pride and pleasure in her classroom management role.

Cynthia is now a junior at East Carolina University.

9

ART IS FUN BUT IT AIN'T PLAY

MY FIRST ONE-QUESTION QUIZ FOR EVERY CLASS EVERY SCHOOL year was always the same: "What is art?" I wanted to lead the kids into discussions about art's role in history, dating back to cave art. Those discussions usually went something like this:

"Why do you think prehistoric man drew pictures on rocks?"

"Because they didn't have paper?"

"Well, that, and because they couldn't read or write, so they communicated with pictures."

"Couldn't they talk?"

"They could make sounds, kind of like animals do, but they didn't yet have a language, so they used art to record images of things they thought were important to be remembered."

My students' concept of history always intrigued me. It was as though in their mind's eye, rather than being a linear continuum, time was compartmentalized into two periods—way back then, and right now, and the way back then compartment was huge.

"Why do you think they only drew on walls inside caves?"

"'Cause that's where they lived."

"Actually, they probably drew outside as well, but those drawings didn't survive the wear and tear of thousands of years of weather elements, like rain, snow, ice, wind. But why did they most often draw animals?"

"Maybe because they're easier to draw than people are."

"Yes, they kind of are, but mostly because they were hunters, and animals were their main food source. In fact, the oldest cave drawing discovered so far is of an animal. Which animal would you guess it is?"

"A dinosaur?"

"No. Dinosaurs were long gone by then. It was a pig, drawn 35,000 years ago on a

cave wall on Sulawesi Island, in Indonesia."

"Where's that?"

"In the Pacific Ocean, near Australia, about 10,000 miles from here."

"Who taught them to draw?"

"They taught themselves. Then they taught each other."

"Will you teach us to draw?" To middle-schoolers, being able to draw is the ultimate art skill.

"You betcha."

"Can we draw dinosaurs?"

To my way of thinking, it was impractical to *do* art without knowing the *whys of art*. Why was so much famous art created in Europe? Why were almost all famous paintings religious in nature? Why were almost all famous paintings created by men?

Those were questions I asked every class of students, to provoke thought about who, what, where, why, and when of prominent early works of art.

"Very few, if any, renowned paintings were created simply to decorate a wall above a couch," I always explained.

"My grandma has a painting of *The Last Supper* above her couch," (or in her bedroom) someone would almost always offer. I cannot tell you how many times I heard those prideful declarations.

"Does anyone know who painted *The Last Supper?*" I would ask. Very seldom did anyone know the correct answer—Leonardo da Vinci.

"Da Vinci was an orphan; no one knew his real last name, so he was named after the town where he was born—Vinci, Italy—so his name literally means Leonardo of Vinci, just as your names could be Roberto ... or Anthony ... or Camilla ... of Oxford."

"If they didn't know his last name, how did they know his first name?" Davina was the first to ask me that. No clue.

Starting the third week of each school year—with the aid of eleven 30-minute-long cartoon-like videos I had ordered the week before starting my teaching career—we began studying the lives of famous artists who either helped invent certain art movements or became one of an impactful art movement's most famous practitioners. We started with Renaissance artists, Da Vinci being the first—who also painted the *Mona Lisa*—and his nemesis contemporary Michelangelo—who sculpted the marble statue of *David* and painted the *Ceiling of the Sistine Chapel.* After that we studied, in chronological sequence:

- Rembrandt and his portrait paintings, the most famous of which is *The Night Watch.* The kids were amazed by its size—as big as one of the walls of our classroom
- Claude Monet's outdoor landscape paintings, including *Impression Sunrise,* from which the word *Impressionism* was coined
- Mary Cassatt, one of the first famous women painters, also an *Impressionist,* and a friend of Monet
- Vincent van Gogh and Paul Gauguin, *Post-Impressionists* who were extremely contentious roommates for a brief while
- Henri Matisse, creator of cut-paper collage art that he called *drawing with scissors*
- Pablo Picasso, pioneer of *Cubism* and creator of those one-eye-in-the-center-of-the-forehead and a-nose-on-the-side-of-the-head-where-an-ear-should-be portraits, like his famous *Portrait of Dora Maar,* his longtime girlfriend
- Frida Kahlo, the Mexican-born *Surrealist* noted for the morbid self-portraits she created after breaking her back in a trolley car accident
- Jackson Pollock, famous for his extremely large pieces of *Abstract Art,* created by spreading blank canvas on his studio floor, then walking around pouring regular house paint on it, directly from gallon paint cans. He called his work *Action Art*

- Andy Warhol, most famous for his *Pop Art* paintings and silk-screenings of Campbell's Soup cans, and for his widely known prediction that "Everyone will be famous for fifteen minutes."

In the end, no matter the school year, nor the middle school grade level, there was

always an uncanny commonality among the tidbits of art trivia that piqued the kids' interest and provoked emotional reactions. Most particularly...

... that Da Vinci, being a scientist as well as an artist, inventing the parachute (which he did) was weird. "They didn't even have airplanes way back then. Did they?"

... that Michelangelo and Da Vinci getting into a fistfight in the marketplace was "Way cool."

... that Monet choosing to paint the same haystack eighteen days in a row "...was just stupid. Why did he paint a haystack even *one* day?"

... that Mary Cassatt having to sometimes forge her friend Renoir's signature onto her paintings in order to sell them because no one would buy paintings done by a woman was mean. "That wasn't fair," the girls declared. The boys wanted to know, "Did she give Renoir some of the money?"

... that Van Gogh cutting off his own ear because a woman he loved didn't love him back was dumb. The girls wanted to know, "What did he do with his cut-off ear?" Some of the boys offered that, "I woulda sent it to *her*." In one class, one of the girls responded to that suggestion with, "Surprise! Happy Valentine's Day!"

... that Dora Maar should have "Kicked Picasso to the curb after he painted that ugly picture of her."

... that Frida Kahlo's unibrow was "Just plain gross!"

... that "Anyone coulda done that," referring to Pollock's drip art. "Yeah! Even I coulda done *that*," someone always claimed. "But you didn't," I would remind them. "But I coulda," they would persist.

10

RINAZAMCE? RENNAZANCE?
RENNASANCE? RENAISSANCE?

MY STUDENTS SUCKED AT SPELLING—THE EIGHTH GRADERS AS much so as the sixth graders—so I announced that I was going to start deducting one grade point for every misspelled word on any and all work they submitted. The kids resisted mightily. I stuck to my guns.

"I'll give the points back if you correct the misspellings and resubmit the work," I promised. "But you must do so within five school days. I'm not going to let you wait until two days before report cards are due out, then bury me under an avalanche of quizzes containing 1,000 misspelling corrections."

I was always struck by how many kids "corrected" a misspelling with a different misspelling of the same word— like Pecasso, in place of Paccaso, instead of Picasso—for which I deducted another point.

Parents also took strenuous exception to me holding their

children accountable for spelling. "It makes no sense; it's just an art class," they said. (Where had I heard that before?)

Several parents took their contempt directly to Mr. Callaghan. He backed me up. "I told them, 'Sorry, but this is a school; I can't tell teachers to condone misspellings,'" he said. Mr. Callaghan was like that.

Our most spirited classroom discussions about the importance of correct spelling—and grammar—always took place on the day I began class with this instruction:

"I want each of you to write down the following sentence: 'There are ... three ways ... to spell ... the word ... to/too/two.'"

Most kids would immediately use the word "two." A few would answer "to." Some would look puzzled and write nothing. And on occasion, someone would ask, "Which way?"

"You choose," I always replied. Rarely did anyone choose option *too*.

Predictably, the kids also struggled with the spelling of certain artists' names. Imagine their distain for monikers like *Michelangelo di Lodovico Buonarroti Simoni* ... or *Rembrant Harmenszoon van Rijn*. They kicked and screamed. Their parents complained to Mr. Callaghan, again.

"Even I can't spell them!" one or two told him.

"Exactly the point," Mr. Callaghan replied.

I also required my students to pronounce the names of artists correctly. On one occasion, during quiz review, Nameishia took exception to my objection of her pronunciation of Van Gogh.

"It's not really Van 'Go' ... that's just how *we* say it. In Holland, where he was from, it's pronounced Van *Gock*. Sounds kind of like you're clearing your throat," I explained.

"Or a cat puking up a fur ball," someone graphically suggested and offered sound effects.

"Big deal," Nameishia replied, and rolled her eyes.

"Oh? But you thought it was a big deal on our first day in this class, when I mispronounced your name, huh?"

The most interesting challenge, though, was engraining the subtle difference between correctly versus incorrectly pronouncing Michelangelo.

"Who painted the ceiling of the Sistine Chapel?" I would ask. (It took forever to get some kids to stop calling it "The Sixteenth Chapel.)

"Michael-angelo," someone would invariably reply.

"Who is Michael Angelo?" I would ask. There would be a moment of silence. "That's not how his name is pronounced; not in his country," I would go on.

"But we're not Italian," someone would offer.

"No. You're not. But you *are* smart."

"Me-cal-angelo?" someone else would usually chime in.

"Is that your answer ... or a guess? I couldn't quite tell."

"Uh ... my answer."

"Good job. You get a Tootsie Roll, for pronouncing his name correctly, and you get a Tootsie Roll too, for knowing Michelangelo was Italian, and you get one also, for being the first one brave enough to offer an answer."

"I know he was from Italy," half-a-dozen kids would then plead, as their three classmates rummaged in the big glass bowl of candy I kept on my desk for such occasions.

"We all know it ... now," I would acknowledge.

"Do y'all realize there probably isn't a teacher in this school who can do that—spell *and* pronounce Michelangelo's full name correctly? But you can," I always pointed out. Smiles would abound.

Full disclosure: I still have trouble spelling Michelangelo's last name—Buonarroti. I can never remember if it is "...rroti" or "...rotti." I even looked it up, to be certain, before writing this.

11

GO FIGURE

WHICH SUBJECT DO MIDDLE SCHOOL STUDENTS DISLIKE MORE than they dislike science, social studies, and language arts ... combined?

Spoiler alert: Math!

Actually, they dislike reading even more than math, but reading is not a subject specifically taught in middle school. It is simply a cruel and unusual punishment often imposed by tyrannical teachers upon their defenseless students. More than once, I passed out one-paragraph reading assignments, only to be asked by someone, "Do we have to read this *whole* thing?"

My response? "No. Just read the important part."

In order to place art in proper historic perspective, it is necessary to understand beginning- and end-dates of art movements, as well as the lifespans of important artists. Ordinarily, that would be an exercise in memorization, but rote memorization does not teach kids to think. As Henry Ford once noted, "I don't even know my own phone number. Why clutter my mind with information I can easily look up?"

As with memorization, I was never a fan of multiple-*guess* quizzes that offered four answer options, two of which were almost always absurdly far-fetched, making it relatively easy for test takers to guess his or her way into a grade of fifty, before factoring in what he or she may actually know about the subject at hand. Fact was, a student could make a grade of 100 on a multiple-choice quiz by correctly selecting memorized choices, yet, know nothing about the how or the why of their answers. I always tried to impress that limitation upon my students, and I always demonstrated it.

"Who discovered gravity?" That was always one of my one-question quizzes. Rarely did anyone know the correct answer. "Who wants to come up to my desk and Google the answer?" There was never a shortage of volunteers.

"Sir Isaac Newton," the chosen one would announce.

"Go write it on the board, please. And spell his name correctly," I would instruct. They would. And I would leave it there for the remainder of the class period before erasing it in preparation for repeating the exercise with the next class ... and the next ... and so on. The kids soon came to realize that anything written on the board would again, at some point, rear its ugly head.

"Who discovered gravity?" That was always the one-question quiz the very next day, offering the following answer choices:

1. Galileo Galilei

2. Nicolaus Copernicus
3. Isaac Newton
4. Albert Einstein

"How many of you answered Isaac Newton? Please raise your hands," I would ask after taking up the quiz papers. Almost all of them eagerly waved a hand in the air. "So your grade on this quiz is what? A 100—right?" There would be clapping and cheering. "How many of you simply wrote 'c' on your paper... instead of writing his name?" About a third would raise their hands, but with less enthusiasm.

After placing their quiz papers in my briefcase, I walk to the board, select a dry-erase marker, uncap it, turn to the board, poised to write, and ask, "Where was Sir Isaac Newton from—what country?" Rarely would there be a response. "When did he discover gravity—what year?" Never would there be a response. I would turn and face the class. "What event made him start wondering about gravity—what it was, and how it worked?" Blank stares would abound. I would recap the marker. "Sir Isaac Newton was from England; the fact that he was a Knight—*Sir* ... Isaac—should have been a clue. And he discovered gravity in 1687. And he got the idea from watching apples fall to the ground from their trees. And he wondered why they fell instead of floating." I would drop the marker back into the tray. "See ... you all got the *right* answer ... but still don't know anything about Newton, or gravity."

That is why, after studying about any artist, or group of artists, or art movement, I gave my students a ten-question quiz. I knew that with properly crafted questions, I could get my students to think and reason and draw conclusions; something 50, or 100, multiple-choice questions would not accomplish. Besides, ten questions usually reached the outer limits of an eleven- or twelve-year-old's attention span.

As a for instance, when we finished studying the Renaissance period (1300-1700), during which we hopefully learned something about Leonardo da Vinci (1452-1519) and Michelangelo Buonarroti (1475-1564), I would give the kids a quiz—I called every assessment a "quiz" because the word "test" instilled them with needless angst—and each quiz included two questions we referred to as "birthday math."

Example:

Michelangelo was born in 1475, which was 44 years before Da Vinci died of a stroke at age 67.

What year was Da Vinci born?

In order to get credit for correct answers, students had to show their work in calculating those answers. Like this:

$1475 + 44 = 1519$

$1519 - 67 = 1452$

Da Vinci was born in 1452

That is a much better, but much less popular, approach to assessment than:

Da Vinci was born in the year _____.

And certainly better than:

What year was Da Vinci born?

1519

1475

1452

1564

As with being required to spell correctly, being required to do birthday math was

initially met with weeping and wailing and gnashing of teeth. But it was a great teaching tool, and fun, because we learned to approach it that way. Periodically, just for kicks, I would include a trick birthday math question on a quiz, such as:

Pablo Picasso was born in 1881

Andy Warhol was born in 1928

Picasso was forty-seven years older than Warhol.

How old was Picasso when he was born?

When the kids got to the trick questions, there would be frantic scribbling ... erasing ... more scribbling ... more erasing ... grimacing ... blank stares ... and puzzled expressions ... until someone inevitably raised their hand and said, "Mr. Massey, I think something's wrong with the birthday math question." Then, we would have a spirited discussion about whether, at the time of his birth, Picasso was zero years old, or one second old, after which the kids chose an answer, either of which I marked as being correct.

As the school year rolled along, the birthday math questions got progressively harder, more complex, and longer, but by-and-large, the kids kept rising to the challenge. And were proud when they did.

12

MANY MORE BIRTHDAYS

OCCASIONALLY, DURING DISCUSSIONS ABOUT THE BIRTH DATE OF one of the famous artists we studied, one of the kids would proudly proclaim, "That's my birthday, too." Jaylen was the first of my students to share his birth date that way. "Picasso's birthday is the same as mine," he pointed out when I included Pablo Picasso in a birthday math problem on a quiz.

"You were born in 1881? That's amazing," I kidded.

"No. I was born in 1999. But on October 25th... just like Picasso was," Jaylen exclaimed.

"So, how old would Picasso have been when you were born?" I asked. Jaylen didn't immediately respond. "I'll give you five bonus points on this quiz," I offered. I could tell he was thinking, but he wasn't speaking.

"I know the answer! I know!" Charlie declared, barely able to remain seated. Of course, she did. She was the class math wizard. I held up my hand to stop her from blurting out the answer before Jaylen had a chance.

"Five bonus points ... and a piece of Bazooka," I sweetened the pot. Literally. I could see Jaylen's interest level elevate. But Jaylen was not a risk taker.

"Charlie, come up here and work out the math on the board, please," I said, holding out a green dry-erase marker.

Charlie jumped up, grabbed the marker, and quickly jotted the math problem on the board: 1991 – 1881 =
_____

"One from one is zero ... eight from nine is one ... eight from nine is one ... one from one is zero—Picasso was 110 years old when Jaylen was one minute old," Charlie announced, no sweat. She filled in the blank and returned to her seat.

"Good job," I said, as I handed her a piece of Bazooka.

"Do I get the bonus points, too?" she asked.

"Is your birthday the same as Picasso's?"

"No."

"Bummer."

I walked over and placed two pieces of Bazooka on the table in front of Jaylen. "One for you ... and one for Picasso ... should he invite you to his birthday party."

At that moment, the kids spontaneously started yelling out their birth dates. As I listened, and observed their excitement, I realized how big of a deal birthdays were to them. They relished the day they temporarily became a year older than one of their friends, or some of their classmates, and climbed a notch closer to "Teen-hood."

During my lunch period that same day, I stopped by Mrs.

Hicks' office. She was our school's database manager. Her daughter Taylor was one of my sixth-grade students.

"Mrs. Hicks, would it be possible, and would you be willing, to print out for me a list of all the students in all my classes that indicates their dates of birth, by month, and their home mailing addresses?"

"How is Taylor doing?" she inquired, before answering my question. She asked me that every time I saw her.

"If they were all like Taylor, I could manage 100 kids in every class," I replied. It was the truth.

"It is possible to print your list. And I'll be glad to," she offered. A dozen or so key stokes later her printer hummed, started chugging, and spit out a three-page list. Mrs. Hicks handed the report to me and I glanced at it; eleven kids had birthdays that month. From that day forward, I acknowledged all students' birthdays by listing their names on the board.

"Want us to sing 'Happy Birthday' to you?" I asked the first couple of kids whose names came upon the list.

"NO!" was the resounding and unanimous reaction.

"Duh. They're too cool for that, now," one of my colleagues pointed out.

That same school year, on Monet's birth date—November 14—I decided to have the kids work in teams of two to create birthday cards for Monet.

"He was an Impressionist, so your card designs must reflect the basic elements of Impressionism," I instructed.

I almost always had the kids work on projects and review for quizzes in teams of two, or groups of four. It was my belief that most students remembered none of what they pretended to read, only some of what I told them, but a lot more of what they were allowed to chat about, or respectfully debate—they called it "arguing"—in class.

Different groups of kids would, from time to time, get what I referred to as "respectfully rowdy." When they did, I would sternly but unthreateningly say to them something my grandma Molly, who raised us, would shout to my younger sister and brother and me when we got slightly off the chain; "Don't make me come in there," and as soon as she did, we would "pipe down," as she put it. I never knew, exactly, what "pipe down," literally meant, but I knew I did not want to find out, even though Grandma never laid a hand on us. Except for that one time she popped me on the hand with her long, wooden stirring spoon after I stuck my finger in her bowl of cake batter. All that did was smear batter on the back of my hand. Bonus!

At the conclusion of the Monet project, we ended up with 80-some birthday card concepts. My favorite—created by Beatrice and Charlene—depicted a brightly colored drawing of a haystack in a wheat field. It was similar to the ones in Monet's famous series of eighteen haystack paintings, except Beatrice and Charlene's version had a lit candle sticking out of the haystack, and beneath the haystack was this clever greeting:

Hay!
Happy Birthday!

As we reviewed and discussed all the birthday card designs, many of my students dolefully admitted that, "I never got a birthday card," which led to a more surprising admission that, "I never got *anything* in the mail."

"Will you please provide me with a quote for printing as many cards like this as you can, for as little money as possible?" I asked of my printing rep friend, Sarah, about a week later. I handed her the haystack birthday card. "But I'll need this back; it's the original."

"Can you give me an idea of a quantity; of how many you really need? Saying 'As many as I can get' to my estimator is a bit nebulous," Sarah asked.

"Well, 500 would be nice," I told her, and told her why I wanted so many. "I want to start mailing birthday cards to my students."

"All of them?" Sarah asked. I nodded. She shook her head and half-smiled. "We can print 1,000 for almost the same money as we can print 500. Maybe ten or fifteen more dollars."

With that being said, I remembered what Sarah once told one of my ad agency client's when he asked how much it would cost to print a marketing brochure for his start-up company. "The first brochure will cost you about $5,000. Each of the others will cost about a dollar each," she had replied, before going on to explain that eighty percent of the expense of any printing job was the cost of the highly skilled labor involved in properly setting up the printing press. "After the first brochure, we're only talking about the incremental cost of ink and paper," she had explained. "A common misperception is that if printing 10,000 copies of something costs $10,000, then printing 5,000 copies will only cost half of that ... and printing 2,500 copies will only cost a quarter of that. That's not how it works; it's not incremental," Sarah clarified.

"Once our pressman hits the start button, the press will spit out 1,000 of your birthday cards in sixty seconds more than it took to do 500; it'll be printing twenty cards per press sheet," Sarah reminded me.

Two days later, I got a call from her. "I have good news, and better news," Sarah said. "Jill Harper—owner of Harper Prints in Henderson—said we will print 1,000 cards for you using cardstock we already have left over from a previous print job ... on the house. *And,* we have some surplus greeting card size envelopes you may have as well, if you don't mind them being off-white color instead of pure white."

"Thanks, but I won't need envelopes. I'd like to mail the cards as Happy Birthday postcards." I had decided I did not want to mail anything that was even remotely personal to any student that was not in plain sight of their parents.

Once I had the printed cards in-hand, I took a few minutes every Saturday morning to sign and address a post-card to each student celebrating a birthday the following week. I wanted to have them in our mailbox by mid-after-noon, when our neighborhood mailman usually made his appointed round.

I did that every weekend, year-round, even for kids whose birthdays fell during our mid-June to mid-August summer breaks. And I continued sending birthday postcards to every student in my classes for the rest of my teaching career. Even when a card was returned marked "Addressee Unknown"— there was a lot more of that, of families moving from place to place, than one might expect—I would quietly hand the returned card to the student the next time I saw them in class.

Once you start something like that and experience the beaming faces when they genuinely thank you for thinking of them, there is no acceptable stopping point.

One day during my lunch period, I was in my classroom entering grades into my grade book when I heard someone quietly call my name. I looked up and saw Bernard, one of my eighth-grade students, standing in the classroom doorway. In our school, there was a lot of pseudo gang activity being perpetrated by kids who were gangbanger wannabes. Some were seventh graders, but most were eighth graders. Some were girls, but most were boys. Some pretended to be Crips. Some pretended to be Bloods. And all "flew the colors" by displaying either blue or red bandanas, until Mr. Callaghan saw them hanging out of their pockets. Gang affiliation resulted in automatic ten-day suspensions from school. Bernard was the de facto leader of one of those gang factions.

"Thank ya for the birthday card," Bernard said, gruffly, trying not to betray his tough-guy persona. I nodded and smiled. He walked away without another word. It was only later that I realized he had chosen to come to my classroom during lunch period so none of his "posse" would see him there and wonder why.

From that day until the last day of that school year, when he moved on to high school, Bernard never gave me another moment's trouble in class. Nor did any members of his "crew." If one of them got out of line, in the least way, Bernard would sternly call out their name, and give them a "Knock it off" look. That was all it took.

Bernard still did not participate in class discussions or quiz reviews, and, out of mutual respect for the positions of "authority" we each were shouldering, I stopped trying to force him.

At the parent/teacher conference following his birthday, Bernard's mother told me, "Bernard has that birthday card on his bureau, in his room. And he told his little brother, who will be coming here in sixth grade next year, 'If you give Mr. Massey any trouble, you're gonna get trouble from me.'"

13

GUMMING UP THE WORKS

THE DAY BEFORE ANY QUIZ, WE WOULD SPEND ABOUT FIFTEEN minutes reviewing. I would call out questions, kids would raise their hands, I would call on them one at a time until someone provided the correct answer, then I would toss that student a piece of Bazooka gum. If a student shouted out an answer without being called upon, they got no gum, even if correct.

"Can I chew it now?" the first recipient always asked.

"Can you? Or may you?"

"*May* I chew it now?"

"Yes, you may, provided...what?"

"I don't smack it or blow bubbles."

"And...?"

"I don't stick it under my chair, or under the table."

"Because...?"

"If I do ... there'll be no more gum chewing in class."

"For...?"

"Any of us."

"Muy bueno," I would sometimes say.

"Huh?"

"He said, 'Very good,'" one of my Hispanic kids would usually chime in.

"Gracias," I would say, and toss that student—the translator—a piece of Bazooka, too.

Confectionery Confidence: Before every quiz, I always passed around a bowl of peppermint candy. "What's this for?" the kids initially asked, knowing everything we did, we did for a reason. "I read that peppermint helps stimulate brain cells, so I figure it can't hurt, huh?" I explained. "Maybe I need two or three," I recall Rufus joking one day. "The article didn't mention anything about peppermint replacing the benefits of studying," I replied.

Tennis icon Arthur Ashe once said, "An important key to success is confidence. An important key to confidence is preparation." (And peppermint candy, perhaps.)

I almost always administered quizzes on Tuesdays, so our Monday quiz reviews could be a reminder to my seemingly forgetful space cadets that the quiz was coming up.

Once everyone had completed the ten-question quiz—seven fill-in-the-blanks, two artists' birthday math problems, and a brief essay question—the kids exchanged papers and we graded them in class. Grading papers in class was one more learning experience. I read the fill-in-the-blank questions aloud then chose someone with a raised hand to write the correct, and correctly spelled, answers on the board. (The opportunity to get out of their seats doubled the number of hands that shot up.)

"Make sure you deduct points for misspellings, including misspellings like t-h-e-r-e, instead of t-h-e-i-r," I would remind them.

"That's not spelling ... that's grammar," an offender might argue.

"In that case, we should deduct two points—one for spelling, and one for grammar, huh?" That usually ended the debate.

If the student at the board misspelled a word, I would loudly shout "EHHHH!" imitating the *Jeopardy* buzzer, and say, "Wrooonnng ... but thanks for playing," then call upon another student. You might think that would be embarrassing to them, but you would be *wrooonnng*. It wasn't, because it was part of our game.

Once the seven fill-in-the-blank questions were graded, kids who volunteered went up to the board and worked out the birthday math problems for all to see.

"Mr. Massey, they didn't show their math work." I could bet on hearing that in every class, every week.

"In that case, their answer is ...?" I would ask.

"WRONG!" the kids would shout.

"Bummer."

"I will grade the essay questions myself," I always reminded. Those questions— "Which did you like most, Picasso's Blue Period work, or his Pink Period work? And why?" for instance—had no incorrect answers, if effort and thought were demonstrated.

Once grading was completed, class captains collected the quiz papers and placed them on my desk, so I could check essay questions and record grades in my grade book. I always kept a manual grade book. (I still have all of them.)

"Why do you do that?" some colleagues—usually the younger ones—would ask. "It's much faster and easier on the computer," they always suggested.

"Because writing the kids' grades in there by hand, beside their names, allows me to *see* and *feel* how each of my students is doing in my classes, day-to-day.

Thoughts on grading and returning quiz papers promptly:

When I was a student at North Carolina State University College of Design, and later at the Massachusetts College of Art, I hated it when professors returned the last quiz two or three weeks later, oft times after they had already given the next quiz. So, I made it my policy to always return graded work within two days. Getting back a good grade is gratifying. Getting back a poor grade is, in many cases, motivating.

The day after every big quiz, I would have a donut from Dunkin' Donuts for every student who had made a 100 on that week's quiz. I knew exactly which donut each of them favored because the first week of class each school year, I passed around in each class a sign-up sheet that said at the top, "Please write the name of your favorite donut beside your name."

In practically every class there would be at least one student who would raise his or her hand and declare, "I don't like donuts," to which I usually joked, "Have you seen a doctor about that?" Some got it, and grinned. Some didn't and looked perplexed. But I always went back to each of them later and asked about their favorite candy bars. Kit Kat and Twix were by far the biggest hits. As for donuts, the most popular among the many, many middle school kids I surveyed over the years was—*drum roll*—pretty much any donut, as long as it had sprinkles.

14

SNICKER SNACKER

THE BOOKKEEPER (A.K.A. QUEEN) AT THE MIDDLE SCHOOL where I taught was an elderly black lady named Shirley Fields. I point out her *elderliness* because she was the only person there older than me—by two months—and I never let her forget it.

Mrs. Fields *hated* it when someone else parked in her reserved parking space—no one else had a reserved parking space, not even the principal—but she *loved, loved, loved* Snickers, She called them "Snicker Bars."

My first encounter with Mrs. Fields occurred about a month after I started teaching, on the morning Mr. Hunt, one of our custodians, unlocked my classroom door with his master key, walked into my first-period class, and whispered to me, "Mrs. Fields sent me down here to keep an eye on these young'uns while you go move your car out of her parking space." I honestly had not noticed the *No Parking* sign.

A few weeks later, figuring enough time had passed to keep me from being suspect, and right after hearing Mrs. Fields complain to Mr. Callaghan that a visiting parent had parked in her space, I went to Walmart and bought a brightly colored plastic toy car that was smaller than a bread box but bigger than a shoe box, and "parked" it in the center of her parking space when I arrived at school the next morning. Several days went by, but Mrs. Fields didn't mention it, not to me, or to anyone else, as far as I knew. About a week later, a note appeared in my mailbox that read: "My grandson thanks you for his new car." There was no signature. And for the remainder of the school year, that toy car was never directly mentioned.

Off and on throughout my tenure as a teacher, whenever I was delinquent turning in fundraising money to Mrs. Fields, I would include a Snickers bar. Sometimes they were fun size, sometimes regular, sometimes jumbo, depending upon the egregiousness of my transgression.

The week before Mrs. Fields' seventieth birthday, Joe, the manager of the Food Lion where my wife Gerry and I grocery shopped, ordered for me a case of regular size Snickers, and graciously sold them to me wholesale.

On the morning of Mrs. Fields' birthday, starting with my first-period class, I gave each student a Snickers and ushered them to the front office. They queued up in the hallway outside her door and, one at a time, trooped into her office, placed a candy bar on her desk, said, "Happy Birthday, Mrs. Fields," and walked out, only to be followed by another, and another, and another, until, by the end of third period, seventy kids, most of whom Mrs. Fields had never met and didn't know from Adam, had presented her with a Snickers.

"Massey, you are one crazy man," Mrs. Fields said to me later that afternoon, when we encountered each other at the copier. "I'm gonna have a cavity the size of a dime by the time I eat all those Snicker bars. But I'm not sharing 'em, with anybody."

"A cavity? You still have your real teeth? Amazing!"

It was well known that Mrs. Fields was a Duke basketball fan to her core, and that her dream was to someday go to a Blue Devils game at Cameron Indoor Stadium. It would be like a pilgrimage to Mecca for her.

One day, in a telephone conversation with Marla, a former client from my previous life in advertising, the subject of Duke basketball came up, and, knowing she and her husband Ed were avid Duke fans too—Ed may even have been a Duke School of Law grad—I told Marla about Mrs. Fields' devotion to all things Duke blue. Not long thereafter, Marla called and said Ed could not use his tickets to the next Duke home game and wanted to know if I wanted them for Mrs. Fields.

"Yes. How much?"

"Free."

Done deal.

The following week, Mrs. Fields and her daughter, as rabid a Duke fan as she, attended their first Blue Devils game, at Cameron. And Duke won. Duh!

A few days before the start of the following school year, I interrupted Mrs. Fields—she was relabeling everyone's internal mailbox cubbyholes—and asked her to issue to me a new fundraiser receipt book. In the process, Mrs. Fields casually mentioned that a couple of our teachers were going to night school in pursuit of PhDs in education, hoping to enhance their chances of becoming principals. "I think I'll do that ... get a PhD ... so everyone will call me Doctor Massey," I remarked, offhand.

The next morning when I checked my mailbox slot for incoming mail, I noticed the label below it read: *Dr. Massey.* It stayed that way the entire school year, and Dr. Carter, our new assistant principal, who was riding out his time to retirement and only with us for the first half of the year, unwittingly addressed me in person, and referred to me in meetings, as Dr. Massey. I never told him any different.

15

SUPPLY AND DEMAND

AFTER COMPLETING OUR STUDY OF ANY ART MOVEMENT, MY kids were assigned to create their own works of art in the style and spirit of that particular movement—within the limitations of the art supplies we had on hand; mostly markers, colored pencils, crayons.

"Why can't we ever do painting?" was always a popular question, with an unpopular answer.

"I wish we could, but we can't afford it. Oil paints, brushes, and canvas material are all very expensive," I tried to explain. (My art supply budget was $150, for an entire school year—less than $1 per student—thus requiring me, or perhaps inspiring me, to spend on average about $1,100 per year out of my own pocket on additional bare essentials.)

Through fundraisers, grant applications, Donors Choose requests, Go Fund Me accounts, and repeatedly and annoyingly hitting-up family and friends for contributions, I begged for donations of money or supplies all year long. That is every teacher's part-time job. But small businesses and cash-strapped parents and neighbors in rural communities can only respond so often. "You can only go to the well so many times," some said. But I was always waiting at the well.

Of course, the expense notwithstanding, I could have more effectively dissuaded the kids' interest in painting by exposing them to the tedious tasks of washing out brushes, wiping off paint tubes, scouring paint pallets, folding and storing easels, scrubbing hands, and explaining paint stains on clothing to disgruntled parents after every painting session. Doing that once would have done the trick, I am quite certain.

Dare I touch the third rail? Oh, why not?

There is always money available for sports; practically never money available for the arts. There never seems to be a realization of, or an appreciation for, the fact that art, music, band, dance, and theater are the "sports" of far more kids than are baseball, football, basketball, volleyball, and soccer. I often raised this issue with Mr. Callaghan, until the day he candidly told me, "I wouldn't touch the issue of reallocating sports funding with the superintendent or school board with a ten-foot pole. They do not want to incur the wrath of parents."

The defense rests.

MANY MINI-MATISSES

I ALWAYS SPENT A CONSIDERABLE SLICE OF MY ART SUPPLY budget on relatively inexpensive colored construction paper and glue sticks. The 8 ½ x 11 plain white paper we used for caricature drawing lessons each week I pilfered from the copier supplies storeroom. (Sorry Mr. Callaghan.)

Drawing With Scissors

That is what Henri Matisse called his cut-paper collage art.

"Why did he spell *Henry* so funny?" was usually one of the first questions about Matisse.

"He was French; that's the French spelling. And he didn't pronounce his first name *Hen-ree*, like we do. He pronounced it *Ah-n-ray*," I would explain, with some difficulty. And it took a bit of day-to-day reminding.

The kids' favorite cut-paper collage project was working in teams of four to create their versions of a jazz quartet. Each team member, choosing between saxophone, clarinet, bass, trumpet, vibraphone, and violin, had to select a different instrument and create a band member playing that instrument.

"I want to make the sax player ... but so does he," or some declaration similar thereto, was a common dilemma.

"Sorry, only one sax per quartet," I would reiterate. "So, figure it out."

"You are going to get two grades on this project; an individual grade on your individual band member, and a team grade on your band as a whole."

"How long do we have to do this?"

"As long as it takes to do it right ... or until I see you have stopped working and started goofing off."

"How will you grade us? How will you know whose project is good, and whose is bad?"

"Art isn't good, or bad. One student's art isn't better or worse than another's—it's just *different*. But to answer your question, I'm going to grade you on effort; on how much time and attention you put into this."

"How will you know how hard we work?"

"By watching you. I am watching you right now. You've had this assignment for twenty minutes, and some of you haven't done one thing to get started. Bum ... mer."

As the jazz band project was winding down, I made the comment that, "A lot of your band characters look like Maynard G. Krebs."

"Who's that?"

"The beatnik guy, from the Dobie Gillis TV show."

"What's a beatnik?"

I couldn't explain it, so I pulled it up on YouTube. It was the first black-and-white TV some of the kids had ever seen.

17

PARENTAL INVOLVEMENT: TWO SIDES OF THE COIN

GRADE EXPECTATIONS

BY AND LARGE, ART GRADES ARE SUBJECTIVE. THAT MAKES grading art difficult. But some students make it easier.

On the days report cards were issued, parent/teacher conferences were held to discuss student performance and behavior, almost always closely linked, for that particular nine-week grading period.

On one such occasion, the mother of one of my students stormed into my classroom with daughter Lauren in tow. She immediately slapped Lauren's report card down on my desk in front of me, and demanded to know, "How did Lauren make a C in in this class; in art, of all things?"

"Let's ask Lauren, since she's standing right here," I said.

We both looked over at Lauren. Lauren looked down at her feet but said nothing. Lauren's mother looked back at me. After a long, silent moment, I flipped open my grade book to fifth period and ran my finger down to Lauren's name.

"Here are three assignments Lauren did not bother to turn in; that's three zeroes."

We both looked over at Lauren again. No explanation was offered by Lauren; none was demanded by her mother.

"Well what can she do to make up the missed assignments?" her mother presumptively asked.

"The assignments weren't missed. They were ignored. So nothing; not now. The quarter is over. She had four or five weeks to do the work and get rid of those zeroes. I reminded her, several times," I explained.

"Can't she do something for extra credit?" the mother demanded.

"You can't get *extra* credit when you didn't bother to get the **regular** credit."

"Well something needs to be done. Lauren is an honor roll student; this is going to keep her off the honor roll."

"I'm sorry, but Lauren didn't earn honor roll in my class; not this quarter."

"Well we'll see; I'm going to talk to the principal about this," the mother threatened as she snatched Lauren's report card off my desk and stormed out of my classroom. Lauren followed close behind, not having spoken a single word throughout that entire encounter.

I never heard anything about it from Mr. Callaghan, and Lauren kept her C.

I Think I Can – I Think I Can

I was in my classroom getting set up for my classes while waiting for the homeroom bell to ring when Phylicia, one of my seventh-grade AVID students walked in looking some-what pensive.

"To what do I owe this early morning visit?" I asked.

"I stopped by to let you know I am transferring out of your AVID class," she said, nervously getting straight to the point.

"Because?"

"Because my schedule is too busy; I can't keep up."

"Okay, but in order for you to switch to another elective class, Mr. Callaghan has to approve it, which he will not do unless I recommend it, which I cannot do unless your mom agrees to it. She's the one who insisted you take the AVID class."

That afternoon, as soon as school was dismissed, but before I left my classroom for bus duty—keeping kids from getting run over by cars, and cars from getting run over by school busses—Phylicia and her mom walked in. I knew why they were there, but I wasn't expecting them so soon.

We sat down at the red table, and Phylicia began stating her case to her mom for wanting to transfer out of AVID class. I sat and listened, like the proverbial fly on the wall.

"Momma, I can't do all the work Mr. Massey requires in AVID, in addition to my other five classes, and be equipment manager for the football team, too," Phylicia said, in summation.

There was less than a millisecond of hesitation before Phylicia's mom responded. "Looks to me like the football team is going to be needing a new equipment manager," she resolutely said.

I still said nothing as Phylicia cried alligator tears and

engaged with her mom in a brief back and forth about the priority differences between what you *want* to do versus what you *have* to do. By the time Phylicia left to go set up for football practice and her mom left to go to a commissioners' meeting, Phylicia was much more confident in her ability to do all that was academically required of her, including AVID class, and all the coach required of her at football practice and at games.

Phylicia went on to do more than was expected of her, and to be one of the best students I ever taught. At the time of this writing, Phylicia was enrolled in college studying construction project management, doing admin work for a district court judge, waitressing at a local coffee shop, modeling, and starting her own fashion magazine. As the kids would say, "You go, Girl."

18

MUSIC SOOTHES THE HORMONAL TEENAGER

I ALWAYS PLAYED MUSIC AT A SUBLIMINAL VOLUME IN MY classes during drawing exercises and art projects work time. A mixture of top 40 pop, hip hop, or country and western, trying to accommodate everyone's musical preferences and peculiarities.

"Turn it up; we can hardly hear it," someone usually complained.

"Huh? What? I can't hear you over the music," I would shout back.

Eyes would roll. But life would go on.

"Mr. Massey, can we play our own music?"

"No. We can't have Jay Z, Led Zeppelin, and ZZ Top all going at once. But, I'll play music you bring in, on my boombox ... if ... the lyrics are age-appropriate."

"We're old enough to listen to anything."

"I was referring to my age, not yours. I'm too old to hear some of that stuff."

"What if the song is about violence, like 'Russian Roulette,' Rihanna's song about trying to commit suicide?" one of the girls innocently asked. I was on the verge of saying, "No, that's not appropriate either," but never got the chance.

"That song is *not* about suicide!" several girls adamantly protested.

"Are you kidding? She comes right out and says, 'Take the gun and count to ten,' then she says, 'Put the gun to your head and pull the trigger.' That is about suicide ... plain as day."

"First of all, the song is about risking her heart, not her life. She never says, 'Put the gun to your head,' because she's talking about taking emotional risks, not risking physical danger."

"What about when she's talking about the guy who's trying to get her to take the gun, and she says, 'That he's still here means he's never lost?'"

"That means he's a *Player;* that he breaks women's hearts, but his heart has never been broken; that he's never lost at love because he's never been in love. So, she knows if she gets involved with him, she'll be playing romantic Russian roulette. But she's going to do it anyway. That's not violence."

"No. It is *stupid,*" someone who had been silent up to that point offers up.

Who said these kids can't critically think?

"Did you know Rihanna's song, 'Russian Roulette,' is not ab...?" I started to explain to my colleagues at the teachers' table in the cafeteria that day but notice them staring at me with "Who?" and "What?" expressions on their faces. "Never mind," I say, and return to my hot dog.

Sometimes one of the kids would bring in a CD, and I would play it to the class.

"I gotta warn you," I would tell them up front, "if there's one word of vulgarity on here, this CD is *mine.*"

Occasionally I played something classical. "I'm broadening your horizons," I would respond to the inevitable, "Why are we listening to *that?*" expression of indignation. At first, they were not all that fond of having their horizons stretched that far, but in time, it grew on them. Well, some of them. "Play that 2001 Space song?" was an occasional request.

The kids marveled at the fact that I could recognize songs by Taylor Swift, Carrie Underwood, Toby Keith, Rick Ross, Beyoncé, Kid Rock, and the like. I did, however, lose some street cred the day I mispronounced Kesha's name.

"Who's singing that song?" Tawanda, one of my eighth graders, tested me when "All That Matters" came on the radio.

"Kesha," I quickly and proudly replied. Everyone laughed loudly, the way only teenagers do when adults screw up.

"It ain't Key-sha ... it's Keh-sha," Tawanda gleefully corrected me.

"And it ain't ain't ... it's isn't," I replied.

Checkmate.

My wife was both alarmed and amazed too, at my pop culture prowess, when I recognized songs on the car radio that were obscure to her.

"How do you know that? Or better yet, *why* do you know

that?" she exclaimed one day when I commented that, "I like this," referring to Train's new pop hit, "Bruises."

"Gotta keep up with the times, so I can be conversational with my little urchins," I explained.

"Yeah, well, you being twelve again is disturbing," she noted.

19

DRAWING ON WHAT YOU HAVE
AT HAND

ONE SUPPLY I ALWAYS HAD PLENTY OF WAS 8 ½ X 11 PLAIN white paper that I pilfered from the copier supply room. So, to make the most of it, starting about week three of each school year, we devoted our Friday class periods to drawing caricatures of presidents, movie and TV stars, sports figures, and other celebrities. I chose to have the kids draw caricatures because, unlike portraits, caricatures are supposed to only *resemble* the subject, not look exactly like the subject; they are supposed to look funny, and in that regard, my students excelled.

I usually started with a caricature of the current US president.

"This is who we're going draw today," I would say, and hold up a photo of Barack Obama, or George "Dubya" Bush.

"That's gonna be too hard," the kids would woefully moan

and groan, practically every time. I would be the one rolling my eyes, for a change.

"Remember ... caricatures are called caricatures because they exaggerate the most noticeable facial features of whomever you are drawing," I would console. "Now, who is this?" I would ask.

"PRESIDENT OBAMA," they would shout. No excuse to yell in class was ever wasted.

"And what's his most funny feature?"

"HIS BIG EARS."

"He looks like Dumbo," someone usually offered.

I always created my own caricature version of the subject ahead of time, to use as a guide, but I did not display mine in advance; I did not want to give the kids a preconceived notion of what their drawing should look like.

While the class captains passed out drawing paper, everyone sharpened their pencils ... in their seats, at their tables ... using one of those tiny plastic manual sharpeners, for one simple reason—it eliminated formation of long lines at our wall-mounted pencil sharpeners where pencils went to die while fifteen minutes of class time was being ground up.

"Can I use an ink pen to draw mine?" someone always, and I mean *always*, asked. Translation: "I don't have a pencil."

"You *can*. But I won't accept it. And you'll get a zero," I would reply, then go on to reiterate that caricature drawing was a process involving lightly sketching the basic outline of a facial feature ... then darkening the feature's final shape ... then erasing excess outlines ... then repeating the process for the next feature. "And you can't erase ink," I would conclude.

Using a black dry-erase marker, I would commence that

exact process on the board, feature by feature. The kids would follow suit, using mine as a basic model. "Remember ... use short, sketchy strokes that can easily be erased later; do not ... do not ... do *not* ... plot your outline in one continuous line, like a computer would."

On the first day of our caricature drawing exercises, before we drew anything, we discussed anatomical rules of thumb for facial feature construction, such as:

- Our eyes are positioned in the center of our face halfway between the top of our head and the bottom of our chin
- The space between our eyes is equivalent to the width of one of our eyes
- The top of our ears line up with the horizontal line of our eyes
- The bottom of our nose is half way between our eyes and our chin
- Our bottom lip is halfway between our nose and our chin.

It always took some convincing that our eyes really are in the center of our face, because we consider our face as being from out hairline down to our chin.

"If you shave your head, then look in a mirror, you'll see that I'm right," I would explain. They would decide to take my word for it.

"As you can see, placement of the eyes is very important, as the first step. Mess that up and you'll end up with a space alien," I would tease.

"Or one of those ugly things Picasso painted of his girl-friend," someone once offered.

"And one of those 'ugly things' Picasso painted was called a ... what?"

"A cubism."

"Close. But not quite. Cubism was the art movement; *cubist* is the art style."

At some point, usually here, I would explain that hand-some men and beautiful women were handsome and beau-tiful because their facial features were perfectly positioned and proportioned in accordance with these guidelines. A proclamation that always resulted in a barrage of shouted-out examples of handsome men and beautiful women, usually initiated by the girls.

"Denzel."

"Brad Pitt."

"Tyra Banks."

"Will Smith."

"Alicia Keys"

"Halle Berry."

"And *me*," I would add. It was the only way I could stop the onslaught of shouts. It worked every time.

As we got deeper into the exercise, someone usually bemoaned, "My drawing's not as good as yours."

"Of course it isn't," I would joke.

"Mine is," someone else would claim.

"Of course it is," I would reply.

"Mr. Massey, come look at mine," kids would periodically shout out. I would walk over, pick up their drawing, turn it upside down, right side up, every which way, and, depending on the disposition of the student, ask, "What is this?" There would be a good-natured chorus of "Ohooos" and "Whoooas" and laughter.

At the end of each drawing class, I would allow all the kids who wanted to, to tape their caricature drawings to the wall in the hallway outside our classroom and leave them there for a few days. It was our art gallery. Every teacher and student in the school had to walk past them, on their way to the cafeteria.

20

READING SUCKS

As I mentioned earlier, many of our students openly and vociferously proclaimed their disdain for reading. Then again, they had never been taught to even *like* reading, much less love it. And that is why so many sucked at it.

On my way home from school one afternoon—it was a forty-five-minute drive—I listened to an NPR radio interview with Clyde Edgerton, best-selling author of a series of books for adolescent readers. He was discussing his most popular book at the time, *Walking Across Egypt*. Something he said— "You can't make kids read without making them *want* to read" —gave me a two-birds-with-one-stone idea.

Every morning, from the time our school busses arrived at school, until the homeroom bell rang about thirty minutes later, all of our students were corralled in the gymnasium and required to sit on the floor with nothing to do but try to stay out of trouble when they weren't trying to get into trouble. As teachers, we hated starting our days with bus duty—babysitting slightly more than 800 hormone-incited tweens and teens for an interminable half-hour.

"Mr. Callaghan, I want to start a reading club. I want to bring kids into my classroom each school-day morning to read Clyde Edgerton's newest book to each other, instead of sitting in the gym, up to no good."

"How many kids?"

As many as want to come."

"You only have what ... twenty-eight seats?"

"Actually, thirty-two, but we're talking about reading a book, not playing a video game; I'll have plenty of seats, believe me."

"Where will you get enough copies of this book?"

"I'll buy them."

"With money from where? There's nothing left in my budget."

"I don't know, yet. Right now, all I'm asking for is your permission to let them come to my classroom as soon as they get to school, rather than going to the gym. Then I'll worry about getting the books."

"Okay. We'll see where this goes," Mr. Callaghan conceded.

The next day I announced to each of my six classes the start of a reading club. I called it a *club* because no one would sign up if I called it a *class*. By end-of-day, I had twenty-nine sign-ups. Not surprisingly, all girls.

That night I drafted a permission letter, to be signed by a parent of all participants, outlining the terms and conditions of being in our club: Be There, and Behave. In the end, twenty-five kids returned signed permission letters.

The following Saturday morning I visited an independently owned book store in Raleigh. I explained my plight to the owner, and she expressed her willingness to sell us thirty paperback copies of *Walking Across Egypt*, at cost.

That afternoon I sent emails to about a dozen of my family members, friends, and former advertising clients, explaining our dire need to raise $225. Two days later I received an email response from Susan, a friend who was affiliated with a Raleigh-based bank, informing me that the North Carolina Bankers Association would be sending a check for $250. The check arrived in the mail three days later.

We kicked off our reading club on the morning of the first day of our new academic quarter, a couple of weeks after our new books arrived. Twenty-three students showed up on day one. Ten days later we had settled down to nineteen participants. One student dropped out pretty quickly, as soon as she realized that, yes, we really were going to be reading every day. I put two young ladies out of the club on day three, when I discovered they had left the gym the previous morning as if coming to my classroom, then hung out in the girls' bathroom on seventh-grade hall until time to go to homeroom. And Mr. Callaghan removed one student from our club for disciplinary reasons known only to him and the student.

Arranged in a large circle, we went around the room each morning with everyone, including me, taking turns reading. A few kids were much better readers than others and were great role models. They read longer passages. Some others, but not nearly enough, read at grade-level. But too many were reading one or two grade-levels behind. They read shorter passages. Everyone was respectful of everyone else's level of reading proficiency, and patiently provided assistance with pronunciation of the more difficult words.

"Can we take our books home, if we promise to bring them in every morning?" Amanda asked, the first day.

"No. This is a team thing. It won't help any of us if some of us read way ahead," I explained. "Besides, these books were an expensive gift to us; we have to take care of them. If a book gets lost, we can't afford to replace it."

Amanda was quiet, conscientious, and made decent grades, despite being woefully behind grade-level in reading proficiency. But from outward appearances, one would never suspect; she had her nose in a book every time I saw her in the cafeteria.

From observation in reading club, it soon became obvious that Amanda had developed an uncanny ability to compensate for her vocabulary limitations. Whenever she came upon a word she did not recognize, she would verbally replace it with a simpler synonym that fit into the context of the sentence and the storyline. For instance, while reading to the group, when she encountered the sentence, "Wesley had a way of getting himself into untoward predicaments," Amanda read it as, "Wesley had a way of getting himself into trouble," without missing a beat.

A week after reading club started, my best reader, Maddie, informed me she was dropping out.

"Why so?" I asked. She didn't answer. She simply shrugged and looked down at her feet. I didn't press her. Being in reading club was voluntary.

Two days later, Maddie stopped by my classroom right after school, acting a tad sheepish.

"My mom said I have to stay in the reading club, if you'll let me come back," she confessed. Maddie's mom was a seventh-grade language arts teacher at our school.

"Muy bueno. Hasta manana," I said, and smiled. I knew she knew what that meant.

Walking Across Egypt is the story of Mattie Rigsbee, an elderly woman who takes in a mangy stray dog, and, much to the chagrin of her adult son and daughter and the local sheriff, befriends Wesley, a juvenile delinquent, when he is released from youth detention.

"As soon as we finish reading our book, which won't be much longer, I'm going to invite the author, Dr. Edgerton, to visit us and read a few passages from his book to us."

"Can we read some to him, too?" Caty, a diminutive Hispanic sixth grader who was also in my first-period art class wanted to know. One had to admire Caty. At eleven years old, she would accompany her mother and father—neither of whom spoke a word of English—to parent/teacher conferences and follow them from classroom to classroom, translating her parents' conversations with her teachers; conversations about her own academic performance and behavior the previous quarter. And she did it with honesty and accuracy. A more daunting and unenviable task for Caty, I am sure, was having to also translate for her parents their conversations with her older cousin Sujei's teachers. Sujei, who lived with Caty and her family, had a lot more to be discussed, shall we say.

A few days later, I emailed Dr. Edgerton at UNC-Wilmington, where he was a professor of creative writing. A day later I received his reply informing me that he didn't usually accept invitations for book readings from schools. "I get so many," he explained. "But no one has invited me to come listen to them read to me from one of my books."

A couple of email exchanges later, we had a date and time for his visit.

"Careful what you wish for; you just got it," I told the kids. "Now you must come up with a plan."

There is a chaotically humorous scene near the end of *Walking Across Egypt* in which practically every character winds up congregated around Mattie's dinner table, contentiously debating the pitfalls of her seemingly blind allegiance to Wesley, and her newly announced caution-to-the-wind plans to legally adopt him.

"We want to act out for Mr. Edgerton the crazy dinner scene," Caty informed me. The others excitedly shook their heads in agreement.

"It's *Doctor* Edgerton," I corrected. That led to a brief and only semi-successful explanation about the differences between a PhD doctor and a medical doctor.

"We're each going to play a character in that scene," Maddie explained.

"And I want to be Mattie," Caty said. No one objected.

Within two days the kids had assumed individual character roles, and, with my permission, had read through the lengthy dinner scene and highlighted, with different colors of Hi-Liter, the dialogue for their assumed character, thus creating individual scripts for each of the nine primary characters.

"The rest of us are going to be narrators. We're going to

read the stuff nobody says out loud," the other kids explained before I could ask.

They rehearsed diligently for two weeks, and performed admirably for Doctor Edgerton, who, after their performance, read to them from the most recent of his books, *Killer Diller*, the sequel to *Walking Across Egypt*, using a different voice for each character. That amazed and mesmerized the kids.

"I want to write a book, too," Caty told Dr. Edgerton.

"Me too," several others chimed in.

"Then you should do it," he encouraged.

"I don't know what to write about," one said.

"Have you ever argued with your brother, your sister, a cousin, a classmate?" Dr. Edgerton asked. Of course, all said they had. "Then write about that; people love reading about conflict and controversy," he noted. "Or, go to any fast food restaurant and observe interactions between interesting people. Imagine what they might be talking about. Take notes of anything you hear them say. I was in a Hardee's restaurant one morning and overheard two men seated in the booth behind me talking," Dr. Edgerton said. Then he went on to recreate that conversation using two different country-bumpkin voices.

My cousin and me went to the creek fishing one day—I love to fish, but he don't care much for it—anyways, I was about to cast my line into the water, not knowing he was standing up close right behind me. When I flung my fishin' pole forward, my hook flewt up his nose, snagged him in the left nostril, and came all the way through the fleshy part; his nose was kinda big anyways. My cousin yelled like a dying cat—scared the bajeezus outta me. His nose started bleedin' like a stuck pig. I tried, but I couldn't get that dang hook out without him yellin' like he was dyin'. He cussed me all the way to the hospital. Then wanted me to pay the doctor's bill.

"I wrote that down, here in my journal, and I'm going to use it in one of my books, one of these days," Doctor Edgerton said.

The kids laughed and launched into a litany of "this-and-that-happened-in-my-family" stories.

At the beginning of *Walking Across Egypt*, there is a scene where Mattie Rigsbee, having forgotten she removed the seat from her favorite rocking chair so she could have it re-caned, sat down in it and fell all the way through the opening, her butt almost touching the floor. She was stuck there for hours, until the dogcatcher showed up and pulled her out. She had called him to come get the mangy mutt who had taken up at her house.

"Where did you get *that* idea?" one of the students laughingly asked Dr. Edgerton.

"It happened to my grandma," he replied.

Dr. Edgerton later told me that when he told that story at a writers' conference in New York, another famous author from up north said to him, "That's what makes me so mad at you southern writers; you don't even have make that crazy stuff up."

"Writing a book takes too long," one of my students whined.

"Well, if you started now and wrote one page a day, in a year, you'd have a 365-page book, now wouldn't you?" he encouraged.

That was the first of three such visits Clyde Edgerton made to our school.

As soon as Dr. Edgerton left, I had each student write on a sheet of paper what she would write about, if she wrote a book, and what the title might be.

"Would anyone like to share with us what you wrote down?" I asked, after I collected their papers. Caty was the only one to raise a hand.

"I'd write about the small town in Mexico where I was born," she said, speaking softly. "My family left there when I was two years old, so I would title my book, 'Things I wish I remembered about Tlaxcala.'"

"Now, please take out another sheet of notebook paper, and write the proposed title of your book at the top," I said. "Then, I'd like you to start writing page one of your book, as Dr. Edgerton suggested. You have fifteen minutes to work on it before the bell rings."

21

NO WRITES MAKE A WRONG

Mid-summer following Clyde Edgerton's first visit, I conducted a two-week writing camp sponsored by the local public library to keep the kids at least somewhat in-touch with writing. Many attendees were kids from the reading club, but just as many were newcomers. A few from other schools, even.

On Wednesday of the second week, heeding the advice of Dr. Edgerton, I took the camp participants on an after-school field trip to the local McDonald's.

"We're going to eat dinner—my treat—and while we dine, we're going to observe other diners and take notes about what we see and hear. Then, starting tomorrow, we're going to write stories about our observations and experiences," I explained, as I handed out permission letters to all fifteen kids. They all liked the idea of me buying them food, but not so much the idea of combining it with "work." That probably accounts for only eleven kids showing up on the day of our field trip.

"Here is a new pocket-size notebook for each of you," I explained as I handed them out on the bus, on the way to McDonald's.

After consuming burgers and fries and Happy Meals, Caty was appointed to come over to where I was sitting with Mr. Tunstall, our bus driver, and ask if they could have an ice cream cone.

"How much is that going to cost me?" I asked.

"Uh ... I'm not sure," Caty replied, after a bit of a pause.

"How much is an ice cream cone—a *small* ice cream cone—and how many of you are here?" I asked.

"They are seventy-nine cents ... and there are ..." Caty said, before turning to count heads. "... there are eleven of us."

"So that's going to cost me ...?" I asked and waited. Caty held up one "I'll-be-right-back" finger and returned to her table where she and Madison and Katrina did some frantic figuring on a napkin.

"It'll cost $8.69," Caty proudly announced when she returned as she slid the napkin over in front of me. I pretended to check their calculations.

"Muy bueno. Now, what about tax?" I asked and slid the napkin back to her. Caty was silent. Her smile waned a bit. "Better go find out. I want to make sure I have enough money," I suggested. She scurried up to the counter.

"There is no tax on food," she exclaimed when she returned thirty seconds later, her smile restored.

I nodded and handed her a ten. "If you kept the change,

how much change would there be for you to keep?" I asked. "No pencils allowed; count it out in your head."

"Uh ... 8.69 ... 8.70, 8.80, 8.90 ... 9, 10—one dollar and thirty-one cents."

"Keep the change."

"I'm using it to buy me a large cone," she grinned.

"I'd like those of you who went with us to McDonald's yesterday to sit on this side of the room and start writing about whatever you observed or experienced that struck your fancy while there," I instructed the next afternoon at writing camp. "And those of you who did not go on the field trip, come sit over here and get busy writing about whatever you did yesterday after school, when the rest of us were at McDonald's."

"Suppose we didn't do anything after school yesterday?" someone asked.

"Then write about what you thought about while you were doing nothing. Or, make something up. Be cre ... a ... tive."

My favorite story to come out of that field trip was Briar's, but it wasn't about anything she saw or heard inside the restaurant.

"On the way there, I saw some buzzards flying in to roost on top of the water tower, like they always do, and I imagined that they weren't really buzzards; that they were remote-controlled drones being used to spy on us by the Russians ... or maybe the Chinese. So, I wrote about that," she explained.

22

YES WE CAN!

On January 20, 2009, we were out of school on a snow day, which was fortuitous; we all got to stay home and watch Barack Obama sworn in as our 44th US president.

When we returned to school from the snow break, my first-period class of sixth graders—almost all of which had watched the inauguration on TV—was abuzz with excitement at having witnessed the first black president take the oath of office.

The demographic of our school was more than fifty percent African-American, so the smiles of hope and beams of pride I witnessed on the faces of my black students was awe-inspiring. You could almost feel the "If he can do it, I can do it" vibe in the classroom.

"President Obama said on TV he wanted more school children to visit the White House," Keana pointed out. I acknowledged having heard him say that. "Can we go?" she asked, taking him at his word.

"I don't know. Let's write to him and ask," I said. Everyone looked at me expectantly. "No. Oh no," I said, shaking my head. "*You* need to write to President Obama, not me."

The kids looked around at each other. Then they looked at Keana.

"Can't Keana do it?" someone asked.

"Yes. She can. And so can the rest of you." There was moaning and groaning galore, then silence.

For the better part of the following two weeks we dispensed with our art endeavors and lit into learning to write letters—a foreign concept to most of the kids—and how to sign them in cursive.

"We're not mailing letters containing misspelled or scratched out words, or grammatical errors," I announced. "Certainly not to the White House; to the president. And we're not writing in pencil either; we're writing in ink, except for your rough drafts. I'll provide each of you with a pen, when the time comes."

"Can I write to Michelle Obama, instead," Brittany wanted to know.

"If you'd like."

"Me too," several other girls chimed in.

"I don't want to go on no field trip. So I don't have to write no letter to the president," Justin confidently declared.

"Okay. No problem," I replied. "You can just write a letter to your parents, instead, explaining why you are choosing not to accompany your classmates on a once-in-a-lifetime visit to the White House, should we get invited," I explained. "Then you can take your letter home, get it signed by your mom or your dad, and return it to me."

"We ain't gonna get invited, no way," Justin grumped, and started writing—to President Obama.

On the first Monday of the second week of February, after a little how-to-do-it lesson, as the other kids looked on, Keana hand-addressed the big manila envelope containing thirty much-labored-over letters to:

President Barack Obama and Mrs. Michelle Obama
The White House
1600 Pennsylvania Avenue, NW
Washington, DC 20500

"What's the NW for?" someone asked.

"*Northwest.* That's the quadrant of DC in which the White House is located," I explained. "So what would the other three quadrants be?" I asked, before having to explain what a quadrant was. After a few heavy hints and some hair pulling, we finally settled upon Northeast, Southeast, and Southwest.

With the properly addressed envelope under arm, Keana and Madison marched it down to the front office, where Mrs. Love, our school receptionist, ran it through the postage meter and placed it in outgoing mail. And the impatient waiting began.

"Have we heard from President Obama, yet?" soon became a daily inquiry. I almost said, "He's probably busy dealing with the recession and the collapse of the housing market, at the moment," but caught myself just in time, when I realized I would then have to explain something to them I didn't understand myself.

Fifteen dog-weeks later, during the first week of June, only a few days before school would be dismissed for summer vacation, Mrs. Love paged me in my classroom.

"Mr. Massey, you have a phone call," she said over the intercom.

"I'm in class right now."

"Then I'll send someone down to cover for you for a few minutes; it's the White House calling." Almost certainly, Mrs. Love could hear the collective gasps from the kids.

Our assistant principal came to our classroom a couple of minutes later, and Keana and I headed to the front office.

"I want you to answer the phone," I told Keana, as we walked.

"What? Why?"

"Because you're the class captain."

When we walked into the reception area, Mrs. Love was all smiles. "I'll put the call through to Mr. Callaghan's office," she said.

"What'll I say?" Keana nervously asked, as we headed back to the principal's office.

"Say hello ... tell him or her who you are ... then listen, very carefully."

The phone buzzed, twice. I nodded toward it. Keana slowly picked up the receiver.

"Hello. This is Keana."

After listening for maybe five seconds, she slapped her

hand over the mouthpiece and exclaimed, "Oh my God! It really is the White House!" I nodded back toward the phone. Keana went back to listening.

"I'm good, thank you," she meekly said, after a few more seconds of listening. "I just turned twelve," she added, then said, "Yes Ma'am," about half a dozen times before saying, "I'd better let you tell Mr. Massey," and handing the receiver to me.

Turned out, the kids' letters had indeed been forwarded to Michelle Obama's office, and someone on her staff had contacted North Carolina Senator Richard Burr's office, asking that they schedule and arrange a visit for my students to visit the White House, and to tour the US Capitol.

Late that afternoon, Cindy from Senator Burr's office did in fact call me.

It was already too late in the school year to raise enough money for such a trip. Also, the kids were in the midst of taking end-of-grade tests (EOGs). Thankfully, sparing me being the villain, our district office made the unpopular decision that our trip must be delayed until at least late August, when school resumed after summer break. That decision presented the kids with quite a conundrum: "We hope summer break *never* ends," versus "We can't wait for school to start back so we can visit the White House."

In the end, however, after my first phone call to Senator Burr's office to discuss pre-trip specifics, it became crystal clear we would not be able to pull off the logistics for our trip any time soon. "At least sixty days prior to your trip, you must submit to us a list of the names of everyone in your tour group—students *and* chaperones—along with their valid social security numbers, to be submitted to the Secret Service for background checks," Cindy informed me. The requirement for social security numbers worried me. I wasn't sure all my Hispanic kids would have one.

"Before you leave school for summer break, I need to know your social security numbers," I told the kids the next day, as I handed out permission letters explaining that requirement to parents. "That gives you four more school days to get your parents to write your number in the blank at the bottom of this letter, and get it back to me," I reiterated. I waited a moment for that to sink in. "Keana, how many school days do you have to get this letter turned in?" I asked, to reemphasize my point.

"Four."

"How many days, Madison?"

"Four."

"Justin?"

"Four." He still didn't sound happy.

From my days in advertising, I knew you had to say something at least three times before most people heard it once.

"Everybody ... what happens ... if I don't have your signed letter back in my hands by next Wednesday?"

"YOU'RE NOT GOING!"

By the last day of school, all but one student had submitted his or her signed permission letter—*all* with social security numbers.

"Oh my God. I have to leave one student behind?" I thought. But my angst was short-lived. The day after school let out, that student's mother brought her daughter's signed letter to school. That same afternoon, Mrs. Love faxed a list of all students and chaperones—there was no shortage of volunteers to serve in that role—to Senator Burr's office.

After determining that it would take at least $5,000 to fund our trip—hotel, charter bus rental, and meal money—I spent the majority of my summer break fundraising. I am certain my family and friends were beginning to cringe when they saw or heard from me.

During my mid-summer "Please help us" letter writing campaign, I decided to write to Bob Luddy, a respected advocate for better educational opportunities, and founder of Franklin Academy and Thales Academy, extolling the virtues of my mission. Within a week, I received an envelope in the mail on the letterhead of Mr. Luddy's company, Captive Aire. Inside the envelope was a personal check for $2,000. No note. Only a check.

Again, my friend Susan also came through in a big way. Not only did CapStone

Bank—the bank she helped co-found—directly donate substantially to our fund, Susan also solicited assistance from the North Carolina Bankers Association. In turn, Thad Woodard, the president of NCBA, through the Association's monthly newsletter, invited member banks throughout the state to contribute to our cause. Almost immediately, Susan began receiving donation checks in varying amounts; dozens of them.

When school started back in August, Susan and a CapStone co-worker, Lauren, paid my by-then seventh graders a visit and presented them with an over-sized cere-monial check ... and a physically smaller negotiable one for more than $2,500 that Mrs. Fields promptly deposited into our "Yes We Can!" fund.

"Be sure to send us a photo of your group taken during your visit to DC, so we can share your experience with our friends and colleagues back here in North Carolina," Susan requested. (That photo was excitedly taken on the steps of the Lincoln Memorial our first afternoon of our trip.)

Expenses for our trip consisted of three major compo-nents: Almost $3,000 for a charter bus, a minimum of $1,000 for the kids' meals, and only God knew how much for hotel accommodation in Washington, DC, during peak cherry blossom season: Enter Susan's husband Eric and his employer Summit Hospitality Group; they donated the use of ten hotel rooms in the DC area, for two nights, including free conti-nental breakfasts.

By the time the kids returned to school after summer break, enough money had been banked to cover the basic expenses of our trip, and then some, but I did not tell the kids. I wanted them to feel a sense of responsibility to help pay for their trip, not simply harbor a misplaced sense of entitlement. To that end, their most effective fundraising endeavor was asking for donations outside the local Walmart one Saturday morning. Even our superintendent was hit-up there for a generous contribution.

Between juggling the White House's tour schedule and Senator Burr's staff's availability and our school's holidays and testing calendars, it took a while to get things arranged. But finally, early on Wednesday morning, April 14th, our bus, laden with thirty excitedly nervous kids and four anxiously nervous chaperones, departed Oxford, NC, bound for Washington.

To lead our excursion, I had drafted the services of my son-in-law RJ, a professional tour guide for Premier Sports, where he was responsible for conducting tours for high-profile clients to major sporting events, including the Kentucky Derby, Daytona 500, Rose Bowl, Super Bowl, and the NCAA's March Madness Final Four tournament. Not a bad gig for a thirty-something guy. "There wasn't much difference between working with your kids and my usual clientele; their behaviors are basically the same," RJ joked, after our trip.

As soon as we arrived in DC, we stopped at a McDonald's for lunch. As each student exited the bus I handed him or her a twenty- and a five-dollar bill.

"Spend it wisely; it's all you'll get to buy your lunch now, and your dinner later today," I warned.

After lunch, we checked into our hotel—four kids per room, and two chaperones per room, directly across the hall. Each chaperone had two student rooms to sentinel. Most of our kids had never stayed in a hotel before, and none had stayed in a room without an accompanying adult.

"I do *not* want to be the one who has to tell your parents you have been kidnapped by space aliens and whisked away to Klingon, never to be heard from again. So, if you leave your room without permission, especially after bed check, you will sit in the bus with me tomorrow while everyone else does whatever everyone else is doing, without you," I promised.

We left the hotel and spent that first afternoon at the

Smithsonian Institution. The kids wanted to see the dinosaur bones first.

"As you leave the bus, I'm going to give each of you $20 for spending money; it's a one-time deal," I told them when we arrived at the Museum of Natural History. "Spend it as you see fit, but, as my grandma always said to me, "Don't spend it all in one place.'"

First thing Thursday morning, April 15th, we reported to the visitors' entrance for our guided tour of the White House. The kids were naively disappointed not to be greeted personally by President or Mrs. Obama.

"I'm sorry, but the president and First Lady are out of the country. I'm sure they would have loved to have been here, if it had been possible," Regina, our tour coordinator, graciously and sympathetically explained.

During the tour, while the adults were impressed by the life-like presidential portraits, the girls were most fascinated by the elegant and elaborate décor—especially the East Room —and the boys were more enamored by seeing snipers on the rooftops and Secret Service agents openly carrying "machine guns" in the hallways.

When we exited the White House after our slightly-more-than-hour-long tour, we were surprised to discover it had started raining heavily. We were acutely aware the bus was parked two blocks away, and the driver had been instructed to wait for us there.

"Keep an eye on the kids, and I'll run to the bus and ask the driver to pull down here," I told the other chaperones.

"Sorry, but they can't wait for your bus here," a police officer stationed in the exit lobby gruffly informed me.

"I guess our fifteen minutes of fame is over," I said, before we all took off running toward the parking lot.

Immediately upon leaving "La Casa Blanca"—as I overheard Roberto say to Carlos from the seat behind me—our bus driver took us, soaked though we were, directly to the US Capitol for our scheduled tour there. That is where the most harrowing but latently amusing episode of our trip took place.

After passing through metal detectors, while waiting in line for admittance into the Capitol building, Garrett, one of our more precocious students, decided that photographing the armed guards at the security checkpoint would be a good idea. He was mistaken. Almost before the clicking sound of his camera shutter abated, two burly men wearing dark suits and one ear bud descended upon Garrett. They flashed their Department of Homeland Security badges and unceremoniously pulled Garrett aside. I walked over in time to hear one of the agents respectfully order Garrett to "delete those photos." Garrett did exactly as he was told, got back in line, and to my knowledge did not speak again all afternoon—something previously thought to be impossible for Garrett. Perhaps teachers' jobs would be easier if we were issued badges, too.

The most enthralling aspect of the tour of the Capitol for the kids was taking turns standing on an inlaid bronze star imbedded in the marble floor of the rotunda that marks the exact geographic center of the city of Washington, DC. Their biggest disappointment was being told, "No, you cannot ride on the underground tram used to shuttle senators and house representatives back and forth between the Capitol and their office buildings a few blocks away." It was obvious they had no desire to see a famous politician.

"We just want to ride a train through a tunnel," they admitted, so I called our bus driver with a change of plans.

"Instead of coming here, please pick us up outside DC's Union Station, in about ninety minutes," I requested, and we took the DC Metro Red Line from the Capitol South subway stop to the Union Station stop—a ten-minute ride. As soon as we got there, I lined the kids up, handed out their $25 meal per diem, and again dispensed a warning. "This is it ... all you'll get to buy your lunch here in the food court, and your dinner later tonight ... so tread lightly."

"Is that something else your grandma used to say?" Jamaal wanted to know.

The chaperones reviewed the wall-mounted directory of food vendors and decided upon four choices for the kids.

"Okay, ladies and gerbils, listen up: If you want to eat at Taco Bell, gather up with Mr. Dickens ... at Pizza Hut, with Mrs. Love ... at Panda Express, with RJ and Elizabeth, my step-daughter, and at KFC, over there with Mr. Britt," I instructed. "And stay with your group. If you wander off, twenty-five dollars will not be enough for a train ticket home."

"What are you going to eat, Mr. Massey?" Keana asked.

"Whatever you buy me," I said. Keana rolled her eyes and walked away with her group toward Panda Express.

While the kids were off getting their food, and before I went to get mine, I walked

over to the seating area and reminisced briefly about that

day almost thirty years ago while I was living in DC, when my long-time girlfriend Sharon and I got together for lunch in that very room, to sorrowfully but civilly break up, and go our separate ways. I had not been back there since.

That final night in DC we ate dinner in the restaurant of our hotel. It was not white linen and crystal and silverware chic, but it was not paper and plastic, either. And the menus were not hung on the wall behind a clerk at a register. The kids actually got to hold them, and try to pronounce words like stroganoff, béarnaise, and tiramisu.

"I'm going to give you a spelling quiz on those words next week," I goaded.

"I will make it worth the extra hassle if you will please give each of the kids their own separate check. They each have their own meal money," I told our two waitresses. "Plus, they will all tip you as well, and with their math skills, who knows how much that might be," I said. The two waitresses smiled and agreed.

"I considered having the waitresses give each table of four students one check, and let them hash out who should pay how much," I casually mentioned to Anthony Dickens, a fellow teacher, and my roommate on the trip.

"Praise the Good Lord you didn't; we've got to go to bed sometime tonight," he replied.

"Okay, listen up please," I requested after dinging my knife against my water glass to get their attention. "Mr. Dickens is placing a ballpoint pen on your tables. And our waitresses are going to give each of you your own bill, so you can pay for your own dinner," I explained. "And remember ... waitresses make a lot of their living from gratuities, so be sure to include one," I said, and waited for a reaction. I got only anxious stares. "What's a gratuity? Anybody know?" No response. "Mr. Dickens, what's a gratuity?"

"A tip," he shouted back. The kids immediately looked relieved.

"And how much should a tip be?"

"Ten percent of your bill isn't bad," he said. He and I had already decided not to overcomplicate the math for the kids; that I would make up the five percent gratuity difference.

"That means you need to figure out what ten percent of your bill is, and add that

amount to your total," I explained. Jonathan's hand shot up like it was spring-loaded. "No, Jonathan, you may *not* use a calculator," I said, and waited for the chorus of moans to subside. "What is an easy way to figure out what ten percent of any number is? We've talked about this before, in class, a couple of times," I coaxed. No one responded. "Keana, how much is your check; your bill?"

"Uh ... twelve dollars ... and seventy-three cents."

"And where is the decimal?"

"Umm ... between the two and the seven."

"If you move the decimal one place to the left, between the two and

the one, it would become how much?"

"One dollar and twenty-seven cents," Keana said after a moment of mental math.

"Now, if you add the tip to the total, you will need to pay the cashier how much?"

Using the pen Mr. Dickens had placed on her table, Keana meticulously did the math.

"It ... is ... $14.00."

"Easy peasy, huh? Do you have $14.00?" Keana nodded, looking relieved.

"Now, I want each of you to calculate your tip and add it to your total ... the same as Keana did ... and write the sum at the bottom of your check. You have five minutes. Then you're going to line up at the register ... one table at a time ... and pay the cashier."

"Will you help us?"

"No. I have to figure out my own bill. But you can help each other. Or you can ask Keana for help."

While the kids were engaged in settling their dinner tabs, I asked the waitresses how much our overall bill came to. They conferred with each other, did a little math of their own, and came back with a total. I gave each of them a twenty.

On Friday morning we visited the Washington Monument, Lincoln Memorial, and Vietnam Wall. Afterwards, before we departed for home, our driver drove us slowly through Arlington National Cemetery. The kids were quieter than I had ever seen them as we rode past many of the 400,000 white crosses and Stars of David.

"In a few weeks, volunteers will begin placing small American flags on every grave, in observance of Memorial Day," our bus driver announced over the intercom.

Later we stopped for lunch in Richmond—at a McDonald's, of course. As the kids lined up to order, one young man, looking like the cat that ate the canary, sidled over to where I was chatting with our bus driver about an estimated arrival time back at school.

"Mr. Massey, I already spent all the money you gave us this morning. Now I can't buy lunch," Ethan mumbled.

"Spent it on what?"

"Souvenirs ... and a t-shirt. When we were at the monuments."

"Well, I guess you'd better go hit your classmates up for a loan," I suggested.

Ethan turned his gaze from me to Mr. Dickens, who had walked up beside me. Mr. Dickens turned up his palms and shrugged, as if to say, "Don't look at me."

Five minutes later, two classmates were spotting Ethan $5.00, accompanied by a mild rebuke. "We told you not to buy that t-shirt, and go broke, Dummy."

It was after dark when we pulled up in front of school. There was a long line of cars snaking through the parking lot. I hoped they were all there.

As the kids streamed off the bus, our driver rapidly pulled luggage from the undercarriage storage compartments. Kids were chaotically matched up with their luggage and paired up with their parents. They said their giggly goodbyes and all were soon departed. Except for Courtney.

I gave the bus driver a gratuity, and he headed back to Raleigh. I divided the remainder of the cash I had between the chaperones, to help offset some of the cost of their meals. Within thirty minutes of our arrival back at school, everyone had departed except for Courtney, Mr. Dickens, and me. He had agreed to wait with me until Courtney's parents arrived.

"Why don't you go into the office and call them, just in case," I suggested. She did. There was no answer.

"They're probably on their way," Courtney said, sounding hopefully uncertain.

Almost an hour later, we were still waiting. At that point, Courtney was obviously embarrassed and apologized every five minutes.

"Try calling again," I said.

"My step-dad answered. He said my mom got called into work at the hospital—she's a nurse—and he has been drinking too much to drive," Courtney reported when she returned to the lobby. I cannot imagine how helpless and abandoned she must have felt at that moment.

"Where do you live?" I asked, trying to conceal my anger at her step-dad.

"In Henderson," she very reluctantly admitted.

I looked over at Mr. Dickens. He looked back. Henderson was about fifteen miles away, in the opposite direction than either of us lived. But that was not the issue. The problem was, Henderson was in another county, out of our school district.

"How do you get to school, and back home each day? Don't you ride the school bus?" I asked, trying to sound conversational.

"Yes Sir. My mom takes me to my grandma's; the bus runs right past her house."

Worried about her well being, but having little choice, we dropped Courtney off at home. Neither of us ever mentioned to anyone that Courtney was illegally attending our school. She had enough problems.

The following week, when back in school, I asked the kids what they liked most about the trip. No one mentioned the White House or the Capitol or the monuments or The Wall or the cemetery. No, the big hits were: "Staying in a hotel room without my parents," "Eating anything I wanted at McDonald's," and, "Having three extra days out of school." But one student's answer surprised me. "I liked being given my own money each morning, and being trusted to manage it all by myself," Gabriella said.

23

FUN AND FREE FOOD

Near the end of my planning period, mostly spent reviewing and grading a perspective drawing exercise—the kids had loved the 3-D aspects of that assignment—I hustled down to the office to check my mailbox.

"Here's a message for you," Mrs. Love said as I passed by her desk in the reception lobby.

I looked at the slip of pink paper. It was from Karin, a friend who worked in the marketing department of Quintiles, a large clinical trials company in Research Triangle Park. There was no message, only a number. I checked my watch. Not enough time to call before next period.

"Our company has a luxury suite at the RBC Center," Karin told me when I returned her call after school. "With the suite comes twenty-five season tickets to the Carolina Hurricanes at-home hockey games. Sometimes we use them, and sometimes we give them away, usually to client companies.

But I can arrange for you to have them to take some students to the game on Thursday night, two weeks from now, if you're interested."

"Duh!"

"How will you select twenty-five students from the 160-some kids in your classes?" my wife Gerry asked. She always served as my fairness barometer.

"There'll only be twenty-two kids; I have to have three chaperones—you, me, and coach Kozak. She's also driving the bus."

"Okay, then twenty-two. How will you pick them?"

"My plan is to reward consistent academic performances by inviting the one sixth, one seventh, and one eighth grader who has maintained the highest overall grade point average, thus far this school year. Then to reward academic improvement by inviting the nineteen kids whose grades have improved the most over the course of this year, no matter their grade level, provided they haven't presented any of their other teachers with ongoing discipline issues."

Karin showed up, unexpectedly, the night of the game. "Someone from our company always accompanies our VIP guests to the games," she explained. The 'Canes won the game. The kids consumed mass quantities of free soda and chicken strips. Most of them actually watched the game, though none of us really understood its rules. And more than one of the kids admitted, "I wish I could skate backwards, like that."

2 4

THE PUCK STOPS HERE

A WEEK OR SO AFTER THE GAME, I ENCOUNTERED AT A SOCIAL event another friend who worked for the Carolina Hurricanes in their PR department.

"All of the kids liked the speed and excitement of the game, but the boys *loved* the physicality; the pushing, shoving, and forechecking," I told MaryAnn.

"And the brawling?" she added, smiling.

"Yeah. That too."

"If they thought the game was action packed, you should take them to see a practice session; the skills drills are amazing. I can arrange to get you in."

"Are you kidding? How many kids can I take?"

"I'd say no more than thirty," MaryAnn suggested. "But you'll need to go soon; the season is winding down."

"How are you going to ..."

"I'm not," I said, anticipating Gerry's question. "The kids' other teachers are going to pick them. I'm going to ask their math, science, language arts, and social studies teachers at each grade level, as well as their electives teachers, to each recommend two students for this field trip," I explained. "But no students who went to the game can go to the practice session," I added.

We arrived at the RBC Center a little after ten o'clock on the appointed morning. The security staff was expecting us and escorted us rink-side. The 'Canes practice was just getting started but they were already hard at it. The kids were mesmerized by pretty much everything going on, but I was most impressed by the goalie's shot blocking drill. The usual starting goalie was "between the pipes," as hockey fans would say, crouched and ready to defend the net. Three other Hurricanes players were positioned at center ice, each with a puck, all prepared to attack the net. When a coach blew his whistle, the three guys with the pucks all sped directly toward the goal as fast as they could skate. When about ten yards away, all three took slap shots at the goal, at the same time, but the goalie blocked or deflected all three pucks—one with his glove, one with his stick, the other with his pads. A-ma-zing!

About forty-five minutes into practice, the action stopped and all the players gathered around the head coach at center ice. The longer the coach addressed the players, the more rambunctious the kids became, until they finally started frolicking with each other at their seats. As the player-coach meeting was breaking up, one of the players dropped a puck onto the ice and fired a shot that hit the thick plastic shield, right in front of us, with a thundering BANG! Everyone— even me; especially me—jumped out of our skins. When we looked to see what had happened, that player skated over grinning ear to ear, pointed to the players behind him who had resumed practice drills, and jokingly mouthed to the kids, "Pay ... attention." Then he threw three or four pucks over the plastic wall to the kids—they scrambled after them like puppies competing for a biscuit—before he skated off to join his mates.

Leaving the kids in the charge of the other chaperones— Mrs. Aycock and Mrs. Brodie, two of the kids' mothers, and Mr. Tunstall, our bus driver—I snuck off to the Hurricanes' apparel store in the main lobby, known as The Eye. My intent was to buy a Hurricanes uniform sweater to give away as a souvenir to one of the kids on the bus ride home by pulling a name out of a hat ... until I discovered they cost $225. Each. I bought a still-too-expensive Hurricanes pennant, instead.

When practice ended, as we were filing out of the arena on our way back to our bus, one of the security guys motioned me over. "If you'll drive around to the other side of the building, to the fenced-in area where the players' cars are parked, and wait by the gate, some of them will most likely stop and sign autographs for the kids," he whispered.

About ten minutes later, the kids were queued-up along a low fence that lined the driveway. About ten minutes after that, players started exiting the parking lot, all driving really nice cars, including one Ferrari and one Lamborghini. Not only did *some* players stop for the kids—*most* players did, including Cam Ward, Eric Staal, and Rod Brind'Amour. That's when NHL hockey became my favorite pro sport.

It is good fortune like that—getting invited to take my students to a Hurricanes practice, being given tickets to take them to a Hurricanes game, as well as tickets to NC State basketball games, performances of *Dream Girls*, *Phantom of the Opera*, and *River Dance*, etc.—that make me keenly aware of the many advantages professional contacts born of my business career afforded me during my teaching career. Advantages not available to many life-long teachers, and most new, right out of college teachers.

25

THE BEST OF TIMES – THE WORST OF TIMES

IN 2010, MY PEERS ELECTED ME TEACHER OF THE YEAR AT MY school. I was surprised and honored. That distinction placed me in contention for Teacher of the Year in my school district, which, should I win, would put me in the running for North Carolina's statewide Teacher of the Year. Wow!

As part of the selection process for district level Teacher of the Year, a committee made up of the assistant superintendent of human resources, two members of the district school board, two experienced teachers, and the previous year's winner, interviewed me, as they did all other school-level winners.

The thing I remember most about that interview was being asked, "What have you learned as a teacher that surprised you most?"

"That no matter how hard I try, and I will give it my all, I will never be satisfied that I have provided these kids with the education they all deserve." I had drawn that conclusion long before that interview.

Short story shorter: I was not selected district level Teacher of the Year.

On the morning of the day the Teacher of the Year banquet was to be held, at which all school-level winners would be honored, Mr. Callaghan called me into his office.

"I need to finish making these copies; my reading club kids will be arriving soon," I said as I impatiently stood in the doorway.

"Please, close the door, and take a seat," he said, as if he had not heard me.

I had not been in a closed-door meeting in Mr. Callaghan's office in months; not since meeting with him and our school's social worker about Kenny, a sixth grader who slept through first-period class, every day, as if he had been anesthetized.

"I hate to tell you this, but, due to budget cutbacks, all middle school art teacher positions are being eliminated for next school year." Mr. Callaghan was not one to mince sugar coated words, but I thought I had misheard him. I had not.

"So, what will I teach next year?" I naively asked.

"There won't be a teaching position available for you next year. I'm sorry."

Talk about being hit by a brick. I simply stood and walked out.

That day—the day I received a pink slip a few hours before I was to receive a Teacher of the Year plaque—was the most emotionally conflicted day of my adult life. It took all day for me to descend from my highest emotional peak, into a valley of despair. "Are you okay Mr. Massey?" I was asked that question a dozen times that day.

When the dismissal bell rang at 3:15, as soon as the students filed out of my classroom, I closed my door, plopped down in a chair at the end of the red table, and got angry. A minute later, I tossed some paperwork into my briefcase, grabbed my jacket, took a swipe at the light switch as I walked past it, slammed the classroom door shut behind me, and headed to my car. That was the earliest I had left school since I started teaching. The busses were still boarding students. All teachers were supposed to stay till four o'clock. "What are they going to do, fire me?" I said to myself.

About five miles from school—as soon as I cleared the well-known cell tower dead zone on Highway 15—I called Gerry at her office. I knew she would be leaving soon to meet me at the banquet site. I wanted to catch her before she did. I had originally suggested that I drive from my school to our home, pick her up, and drive back to the banquet, together.

"No. That's silly. That's an extra seventy miles for you to drive. I will meet you there," Gerry had offered. "I know where the banquet is; right down the road from your school, at West Oxford Elementary, right?"

The first time I called, she didn't answer. When I called again, five minutes later, she immediately picked up. "Sorry. I was on another line when you called earlier," she explained, before asking, "Excited about the banquet?"

"I'm not going," I snapped. There was a long moment of silence.

"Why not?" she finally asked. I told her, using a few well chosen, minimal-letter words.

"You *cannot* simply blow off the banquet, leaving your school unrepresented and Mr. Callaghan in a lurch. That would not be fair to your fellow teachers. They elected you Teacher of the Year for *this* year ... not *next* year."

"I'm already halfway home."

"I'm sure there are places you can turn around and go back."

Forty-five minutes later I was back at school, changing into my navy-blue suit, white shirt, and Wolfpack-red tie. By then it was 5:30 p.m. The sit-down-dinner banquet was scheduled to commence at six o'clock.

Gerry and I stayed at the banquet no longer than I had to, which was a lot longer than I wanted to. It was an awkward experience for her, for me, and for Mr. Callaghan—he and I barely spoke to each other—and to add insult to injury, the assistant superintendent, the same person who had eliminated my job, was the one who presented me with my plaque, and sang my praises to attendees.

At that point, there was a month left in the school year; a long time for me to conceal my dismay from my students. Fortunately, most of that time was consumed by core subject review, exams, and end-of-year testing—a period when no one is overjoyed, so I didn't stand out. I didn't know whom Mr. Callaghan had told about my plight, but the only person I told was my friend and fellow teacher, Boyce. "Aren't you glad you teach *science?*" I insensitively joked.

For quite some time before this all unfolded, I had been entertaining a brainchild; development of a course in which middle school kids would be taught how to learn—and like it. To that end, I spent two weeks putting flesh on the skeleton of that notion and putting it into presentation form. On the Monday of the last week of the school year, I informally made my pitch to Mr. Callaghan.

"I could teach six classes per day, just as I do now—two sixth-, two seventh-, and two eighth-grade classes. I could teach the kids how to *hear* when they listen, how to *see* rather than stare when they look, how to take notes effectively, how and why to behave and be respectful, how to *think* before they speak or *do*, how to work in groups as part of a team, and how to have *fun* in a classroom without having to disruptively play. I could teach them to be better students *and* better, nicer people. That's it, in a nutshell."

"All well and good, but if I had budget money to pay you to teach that, I could use it to pay you to teach art," Mr. Callaghan replied in a resigned tone.

"I'll do it for half-pay, and I'll use art as a teaching tool for all the other stuff I mentioned. Two birds, one stone," I offered, having already considered that as a probability.

"I don't have half-pay. I have nada."

"Then I'll do it for nada, until times get better."

"I can't ask you to do that, and central office probably won't allow it."

"You didn't ask; I offered. And if you'll agree to endorse it, it'll be up to me to convince the powers that be."

Two days later—Wednesday—I made a more formal pitch for my program to the superintendent and assistant superintendent of human resources.

"I call my program *Love2Learn*," I said, to close my presentation.

"How many students could you have in each of your six classes?" the superintendent asked.

"I have thirty-two seats in my classroom, so thirty-two."

"How many students do you think will be interested in this, as an elective," he followed up.

"They'll be required to *work*, and to *behave*, so none, at first. But, if I conduct information meetings over the summer break to explain the advantages of the program to parents, they will enroll their kids—kicking and screaming and scratching and clawing, no doubt, but the kids will learn to love it."

"Mr. Callaghan said you offered to do this ... to teach this class ... for free," the assistant superintendent said.

"I did."

"Are you crazy?" the superintendent asked.

"I am."

"I can't allow you to be in the classroom, not long term, unless you are a paid school system employee, and I can only afford to pay you as a permanent sub—$1,250 a month, gross pay," he offered.

"That beats sitting home watching *Oprah*, *Dr. Phil*, and *Ellen*," I half joked. He didn't laugh. Or smile, even.

Over that summer, I conducted four parent information sessions; two at noon for parents who worked nights, and two at seven p.m. for parents who worked days. "I want to help your children become successful students." That was my basic commitment. By the time school started back on August 25th, I had twenty-eight students in each of my six *Love2Learn* classes.

About halfway through the second quarter of that school

year, right after our Thanksgiving break, I got a phone call from a reporter for our local CBS-affiliated TV station.

"As I understand it, you were Teacher of the Year at your school last year ... but on the day of the awards banquet, you were fired because of budget cuts. Is that correct?" the reporter asked.

"Well, not to put too fine a point on it, but I was *furloughed.*"

"Would you mind if I came to your home, to interview you?"

"It will have to be in the evening," I said. She agreed.

At 7:00 p.m. the next night, I sat in one of the matching wing-back chairs in our living room and the reporter sat in the other while a cameraman sat on our couch videoing our thirty-minute conversation about the impact teachers have upon the lives of their students, and the impact budget cuts were having upon the lives of teachers.

"Is it true that you are teaching, full time, in a North Carolina public school, for no pay?" the reporter asked.

"Actually, they're paying me sub pay."

"What an unlicensed substitute teacher would be paid ... correct?"

"Correct. Twelve thousand five hundred dollars a year."

"How does that compare to your regular pay; to what you were making before? Before you were *furloughed*?"

"Nigh onto one-fourth."

"How do you think your principal feels about this oxymoronic situation?"

"You'd have to ask him."

On Friday, the same reporter and cameraman were at my school, interviewing Mr. Callaghan.

The following Monday, the story—edited down to two minutes—aired on the evening news. The crux of the story boiled down to Mr. Callaghan's answer to the reporter's final question: "How do you explain firing your Teacher of the Year, simply to save money?"

"When it comes to budget-cut staff reductions, it doesn't matter *how* you teach so much as *what* you teach," Mr. Callaghan explained.

Three weeks later, when we returned to school following Christmas/New Year's break, Mr. Callaghan shared with me an email he had received that day. He was told to inform me that, "Starting second semester, Mr. Massey's salary will be restored to full pay. To what he was being paid last year."

"But there won't be any back pay. I asked," Mr. Callaghan said, apologetically.

Seems the chairman of the school board had seen the story on the evening news and had expressed his displeasure with the negative publicity to the superintendent.

None of the art positions in the other middle schools in our district were reinstated, and I never returned to teaching art at my school, but rather continued to teach *Love2Learn*, using art as a platform in lesson planning.

26

LEARNING TO LOVE TO LEARN

"MY SEVENTH- AND EIGHTH-GRADE CLASSES CAN BE COED, BUT I'd like my two sixth-grade classes to be gender-specific." That was my request of Mr. Callaghan as we prepared the schedules of my first-ever *Love2Learn* (L2L) classes.

"It's a known fact that boys and girls learn differently, so why not try to accommodate that; to take advantage of it?" I asked.

"Parents will pitch a hissy fit," Mr. Callaghan predicted.

"Parents were told we would do things differently in L2L; they even signed contracts agreeing to support it."

"The kids will have a conniption."

"Of course, they will. They're eleven or twelve years old. And this is *school.*"

When all was said and done, I wound up with a first-period class of thirty-one girls, and a second-period class of twenty-seven boys. The girls noticed the absence of boys the first day but didn't complain. It was day three, or four, before the boys picked up on it enough to react. "Hey! There's no girls in here," one of the boys exclaimed.

"Duh!" several others responded, in unison.

Not one parent raised the issue of our all-girls and all-boys rosters, until our first parent/teacher conferences, where all comments were supportive.

The experiment was quite eye opening. Girls were innately more low-key. Yes, they talked in class, but to the other girls at their tables. Boys were more high-strung. They talked in class too, by shouting to classmates on the other side of the classroom.

Note: Initially I used the words *passive* to describe the in-class demeanor of girls, and *active* as the descriptor for boys. My wife took exception. She maintained that "passive girls" seemed critical, where as "active boys" sounded complimentary. That was not my intent. I was going for "opposite, but equal," not "bad and good," or "worse and better." We mutually settled upon "low-key" and "high-strung."

Boys were also more fidgety. They were quite fond of wadding up the smallest of scraps of paper, or whole sheets of perfectly good notebook paper, then walking over and tossing it into a wastebasket before strolling back to their seats as slowly as possible, unable to resist the urge to shove or playfully punch or frolic with a classmate along the way. I solved that problem by placing both of our wastebaskets in close proximity to my desk. Having to walk right up to me to do that seemed to lack appeal.

From my conversations with some of the girls, and from conversations between them that I overheard, I learned that they liked having a class period where they didn't have to be "on their game," trying to impress boys; a period during which they could "let their hair down," literally and figuratively.

The boys, on the other hand, were much less vocal about the absence of girls, but by comparison to my other four coed classes, it was obvious the gender-segregated boys were much more participatory in class, and far less afraid of saying something "stupid," or asking a "dumb question." Nor were they compelled to show off.

27

NBA, NFL, OR BUST

IT WAS AMAZING TO ME HOW MANY OF THE BOYS IN MY CLASSES already had their futures figured out—almost all were going to play pro basketball or football, or both—so getting an education was little more than an inconvenient nuisance to them.

"In order to do that ... get drafted ... you will have to graduate from high school *and* from college," I coaxed.

"LeBron didn't go to college!" was always their emphatic retort.

"How many people are there on earth?" I would ask. They had no clue. "Seven ... billion. That's a seven ... followed by nine zeroes. Who wants to go write that number on the board?" I would ask. Two or three boys would raise their hands—any excuse to get out of their seats—and I would let them all do it.

"Now ... how many LeBron James' are there on earth?" I

would ask. "ONE," I would immediately add while holding up one finger, to make my point.

On one such occasion, a group of the boys seemed so resolute in their confidence of playing basketball at UNC, Duke, NC State, or Davidson (due to Stephen Curry's sudden popularity), and then in the NBA, I wrote to the basketball coaches of all four of those colleges, soliciting moral support:

Dear Coach Williams, (or Krzyzewski, or Lowe, or McKillion)
Good news! Practically every boy in my middle school classes will
soon be coming to play basketball for you, as a stepping stone to the
NBA ... despite the fact that many aren't doing very well in school
here, and most don't even play on our middle school basketball team.
What should I tell them?

I never heard back from three of those coaches, but within a month, my students got a cordial, encouraging, but candid full-page letter from the fourth coach, the gist of which was:

Dear students –
I would welcome the opportunity to coach you, to have you on my
team, provided you demonstrate your abilities there in middle
school, in the classroom, as much so as on the basketball court.
Sincerely,
Roy A. Williams, head basketball coach

University of North Carolina at Chapel Hill
After I read Coach Williams' letter to my students, and let them pass it around, let them *feel* it, Mr. Callaghan read it to the entire school over the PA system during morning

announcements. Then we had it framed and hung in the front lobby.

I am an NC State grad; thus, I am not a Tarheel fan. But I am a Coach Williams fan.

The day after we received and read Coach Williams' letter, we discussed in every class period the overarching point I thought Coach Williams was trying to make.

"You cannot simply *be* a pro athlete ... or veterinarian ... or doctor, lawyer, Indian chief ... or teacher (trust me on that one). You have to *become* them. And the time to start becoming them is right now," I said. "That is your job at this stage of your lives. Your *only* job."

"Then why don't we get paid?" one smart-alecky boy laughingly asked. I gave him the kid-friendly CliffsNotes explanation of deferred compensation, to no apparent avail.

During homeroom the next morning, after taking role, while waiting for the first-period bell to ring, I wrote, "Do what you have to do now, so you can do what you want to do later," at the very top of the whiteboard. Practically every one of my homeroom students stopped fidgeting and squirming long enough to watch me, but when I was finished, not one of them asked about it. Curiosity was a rare condition among middle schoolers.

"Jeremy, what does that say?" I asked as I dropped the dry-erase marker into the tray and habitually brushed my hands together as if removing non-existent chalk dust. Jeremy read it. The dismissal bell rang. I let it go at that and dismissed them.

Do what you have to do now, so you can do what you want to do later.

At the beginning of practically every class period for the remainder of that school year, I had someone—usually the one paying the least attention at the time—read that anthem aloud.

A few weeks later, my friend and teaching colleague, Terry —a UNC grad, huge Tarheel fan, and Roy Williams disciple— came to me with an idea.

"I know somebody who knows Julius Hodge, personally. Julius does a lot of charitable work for underprivileged kids. I would bet he would come and speak to our students, if my friend asks him," Terry suggested.

At that time, Julius was playing in the NBA for the Denver Nuggets. Before that, he played at NC State where he was a jersey-in-the-rafters superstar in the early 2000s.

Terry called his friend, who called his friend, who called Julius. Plans were made, and sure enough, when his schedule permitted, Julius paid our students a visit.

By the time Julius arrived at our school, about mid-morning on the appointed day, Mr. Callaghan had assembled our entire student body—800+ kids—in the gymnasium. Terry introduced Julius— "Number 24, The Harlem Jule," Terry said—and Julius launched into entertaining and encouraging the kids. He was quite the showman, with an ever-present, mischievous grin.

Almost immediately, when Julius noticed a young man in the front row chewing gum, he stopped in mid-sentence, walked over and whispered—into the microphone— "Are you supposed to be chewing gum in here, around this hardwood floor?" The boy smiled sheepishly and shook his head. "Didn't think so," Julius replied, fist-bumped with the kid, and went back to his schtick.

About halfway into his talk, when two boys seated about halfway up the bleachers got a bit rowdy with each other, Julius stared at them in silence for a very long uncomfortable moment. Everyone, except the two boys, went stone cold quiet. The boys didn't notice and kept frolicking.

"Yo! You in the red jacket ... and you in the green hoodie!" Julius calmly called out, again using the mic. The two disruptors noticed they had become the center of attention. "Have you two gentlemen finished middle school?" Julius asked, in a solemn tone. He got no response. "Have you graduated from high school ... and from college?" No response. "Have you ever been ACC Player of the Year? Or played in the NBA?" Dead silence. "I have," Julius admitted. "So I'm the entertainment here," he added, then waited a moment before breaking into his patented ear-to-ear bright-toothed smile. The gym erupted into laughter and applause. Julius curtsied.

During his off-season summers, Julius conducted a popular week-long basketball camp in Raleigh. I was aware of a family with four children, three girls and a boy, all under the age of eleven. The boy, Jaylen, was a huge basketball fan. Duke was his favorite college team, but that was subject to change. The father, Dietrich, was unemployed. The mother had a working-poor-waged job in a nursing home. Their kids were as adorably polite, well behaved, and happy as anyone could imagine. I mentioned Jaylen to Terry one day at school.

"I'll talk to Julius about Jaylen attending his basketball camp this summer," Terry offered. At that point, Terry had

Julius' cellphone number. Within days, he had discussed Jaylen's situation with Julius.

"We know Jaylen is a year shy of your published age range," Terry admitted.

"Not a problem. We'll take good care of him," Julius assured him.

"Bill and I will pay Jaylen's attendance fee."

"I'll settle for half, to cover out-of-pocket expenses."

That summer, I picked Jaylen up each morning and took him to Julius' camp. He had a wide-eyed blast—especially the day his dad went with him and proudly watched every bounce of the ball from the bleachers.

BUT WAIT, THERE'S MORE

OUR DISCUSSIONS ABOUT COACH WILLIAMS' LETTER AND THE connections he pointed out between education and athletics led me to an alarming realization: That beyond Duke University in Durham, The University of North Carolina in Chapel Hill, NC State University in Raleigh, and Davidson University, my students, regardless of gender or grade level, knew very little about the existence of any other colleges or universities.

The following Saturday, intent upon nudging them outside their small bubbles of college awareness, I went to the student supply stores at both Saint Augustine's University and Meredith College, both located near my home, and purchased, in my size, a t-shirt emblazoned with their respective names and logos.

That Monday, I wore my new grey-with-dark-blue-lettering Saint Augustine's—St. Augs, as they say—t-shirt to school.

"From looking at this t-shirt, what can you tell me about this school?" I asked each class. A few students had, "Heard of it." Most had not.

"What do you think this acronym ... HBCU ... means?"

After briefly addressing, "What's an acronym?" I explained that HBCU stood for *Historically Black Colleges and Universities.* "For many years, Saint Agnes Hospital, which was located on the Saint Augs campus, was the only hospital between Washington, DC, and Atlanta, Georgia, that would admit black patients," I pointed out.

"Suppose it was an emergency?" someone in third period asked. Good question.

The next Monday I wore my pink-with-maroon-lettering Meredith College t-shirt.

"You look funny in a pink t-shirt," Allison said, in first period.

"Why is that?" I asked.

"It's a girl's color."

"So why would their school colors be pink and maroon?" I asked. Kristie raised her hand, hesitantly.

"Because it's a ... a girl's school?" she said, with a questioning tone.

"It started out that way and remained an all-women's college for more than 100 years. But a few male graduate students are enrolled there now."

"Ooo!" a couple of the girls protested.

"What are you doing? And who are you mailing all those letters to?" Gerry asked on Sunday afternoon, as the printer on my desk at home buzzed, hummed, dinged, and clattered away. (It was ancient; on its last leg. I had taken it when the last ad agency I had worked for got new ones.)

"They're letters to the presidents or chancellors of all the ACC and all the Ivy League colleges and universities."

"Going back to school, are you?"

"I'm begging for the donation of one of their school's t-shirts, in my XL size. I want to get enough to wear a different college's shirt every Monday for the remainder of the school year, to expand the kids' awareness of other schools outside North Carolina."

"Free shirts? Good luck with that," Gerry said.

To hedge my bets, over the next couple of months, using my school's letterhead, I also wrote letters—twenty-five every Sunday afternoon—until I had solicited a t-shirt from the heads of the 200 largest or most well-known colleges in the US. And, on a lark, I asked for one from Sorbonne University in Paris. (France. Not Texas.)

Every Monday morning, Mrs. Fields would run my letters through the postage meter and drop them in the outgoing mail.

With that endeavor concluded, and with the realization that not every kid wanted to—or could afford to—go to a four-year college, I wrote similar letters to the head administrators of the 100 most popular junior colleges and technical trade schools in the country.

"How many is that, now—300 letters, in total?" Gerry asked.

"And twenty-three—323. I'm hoping for a ten percent return."

Within a few weeks of sending out my first batch of letters, I had received t-shirts from all eight Ivy League schools. In fact, Harvard sent two—an XL for me, and a SM for a student. Additionally, eleven of the ACC schools—there were only twelve at that time—had provided a t-shirt, and several sent school pennants. As for the one ACC holdout—I won't say which one, but Thomas Jefferson would have been sorely disappointed—the chancellor went so far as to write back to me, explaining that, "Our university does not promote itself in this manner." He had completely missed the stated point of my efforts: "It is my hope to promote the value of higher education in general, and to create an awareness among my students of particular colleges and universities outside our state," I had tried to explain.

Not to be deterred, I scribbled a handwritten note at the bottom of the chancellor's letter saying, "Then perhaps you would be willing to sell me a shirt," and returned it to him, along with a personal check for $20 made out to the university. Within a few weeks, he had someone mail to me a t-shirt. And he had my check deposited.

By the time the dust settled from my whirlwind of letter writing, I had received 232 t-shirts from the 323 colleges, universities, junior colleges, community colleges, and trade schools I had contacted. To store them, I had to install a long, makeshift galvanized pipe clothes rack, and buy enough wire hangers from my local dry-cleaners, to store them all in our basement at home.

Thereafter, for a school-year-and-a-half, I wore a different college's t-shirt to school ... every day. And every Monday I would ask each class, "Who can name one of the colleges whose shirt I wore last week?" When hands went up, I would choose someone to go write the name of one of the colleges on the board. If they were correct, and had spelled it correctly, they got to fetch a Tootsie Roll—I had decided to switch from Bazooka gum, for a while—from the big bowl on my desk. Then, another student would go write another name on the board, until we had listed them all for the week.

29

A SHIRT OF THEIR OWN

"THAT SHIRT IS SOOO WAAAY COOL. WHY CAN'T WE HAVE OUR own t-shirt?" Charlie, one of my seventh-grade girls, asked the day I wore the neon-green t-shirt with glow-in-the-dark yellow lettering sent to me by the University of Oregon.

"Our school already has a t-shirt," one of the boys replied.

"That's not a school shirt ... it's a sports shirt," another of the girls chimed in. "It says *NGMS Knights* ... right on the front ... plain as day."

"Yeah! And we're not talking about a school shirt, anyway. We want our own shirt for *Love2Learn*," Charlie emphatically explained in a surprisingly prideful statement of support for academics. I figured I should strike while the iron was hot.

"How do you propose we pay for a shirt for every L2L student?" I asked. "There are 168 of you."

"Pay how much?"

"I don't know. But I have a neighbor, John, who's in the t-shirt printing business. You can call and ask him," I suggested. "But when you do, John will want to know how many shirts you need in each size."

That night when I got home I spoke with John. He gave me a color chart showing the ten colors in which his recommendation for a reasonably priced but durable t-shirt was available.

"Call me with a color choice and a breakdown of sizes, and I'll give you a price," John said.

The following morning, using a blank student roster for each class, Charlie prepared a sign-up sheet, with a handwritten, to-the-point note at the top of each.

Beside your name, write what size t-shirt you wear and which color you like best for a L2L t-shirt. And write so we can read it.

I had her add *Please* at the end.

We passed the color chart and third-period sign-up sheet around then and there. I

also passed them around in my last three classes of that day, and the first two classes the next morning.

"Here are the t-shirt sign-up sheets for all six classes. Pick someone to assist you in tallying them up, by size. Also determine which color choice got the most votes," I said to Charlie when she came to class later that morning. She chose Joy to help her. In about twenty minutes, the two of them were back at my desk.

"Here's our list," Charlie said. I looked it over.

"Three kids were absent yesterday, but I'm guessing one would wear a small and

two would wear mediums. So, add those to your list," I

said. Charlie erased and scribbled, erased and scribbled, and handed the list back to me.

XSM- 5

SM- 16

M- 65

L- 55

XL- 24

XXL- 4

Total- 169

"We added an XXL for you," Joy said, when she saw me looking at the total.

"I wear an XL, I'll ... have ... you ... know," I said, grinned, and handed her the

list.

Oops!" Joy said, before erasing and scribbling some more.

"What about color choice?"

"This is it ... the kinda blue-green one," Charlie said, pointing to the chart. "They call it *teal*. That one got the most votes."

"Yeah, by a lot. The tick marks, where we counted, are on the back, if you want to see 'em," Joy said.

"And we want white lettering," Charlie chimed back in.

"Me and Charlie decided that ... about the lettering ... on our own," Joy piped up again, sounding proud and definitive.

"'Me and Charlie?' Is that the same as Charlie and I?" I asked.

That evening I gave John the list of sizes and told him the color choice. "Call me tomorrow. I'll have a price," he promised.

The next morning, I arranged with Mrs. Love for Charlie

and Joy to come to the front office during our class period and use a phone to call John.

"Here is Mr. Perceval's phone number. Take a pencil and paper to take notes," I suggested. Joy proudly held up the pen and pad she already had in her hand. "Mrs. Love is expecting you."

The two of them left the classroom nervously giddy. Fifteen or twenty minutes later they were back, looking much more confidant.

"John said—he told us to call him John—John said it will cost us $588, and ..." Charlie was saying.

"And it will only take five business days to get our new shirts," Joy excitedly interrupted.

Charlie waited impatiently for Joy to finish before continuing, "... and he's only going to charge us the cost of the shirts. And he'll do the printing ... uh ... uh ..." Charlie said, then looked over at Joy, expectantly.

"... gratis?" Joy quizzically added.

"That's a Latin word. It means, 'At no charge.' He's going to do the printing for free," I explained. The two of them stared at me for a moment. I knew they were thinking, "Then why didn't he say *that*?"

Gerry suggested she and I donate $100 to the cause, and Mr. Callaghan contributed $100 from his discretionary budget. The kids collected a total of $276 from their families and friends, and they sold $185 worth of Krispy Kreme fundraiser donuts.

"That's $661," Charlie pointed out. "John said it would only cost us $588. So, we'll have a bunch of extra money."

"But we also have to pay seven percent sales tax," I told

her. "How much is seven percent of $588? Go to the board and figure it out."

"Right now?"

"Yes. Right now, without a calculator. And don't forget to put a zero in front of the seven, and the decimal in front of the zero, when you multiply."

"No ... kidding," Charlie said, with mock resentment at my unneeded tutelage.

She strutted to the board and set about multiplying and adding and carrying remainders until she came up with, "The tax is $41.16, which means we will owe John $629.16. So, we will still have $31, and something, extra."

"And *something*? How much money is *something*?" I asked. "If you had two dollars and fifty cents, and you wanted to buy a cone of ice cream, and the clerk said, 'That'll be two dollars and *something*,' how would you know if you had enough to pay for your ice cream?"

After some subtraction, Charlie said, "We will have $31.84 extra."

"Isn't ... that ... *something*?" I said. Charlie rolled her eyes and returned to her seat.

A little over a week later, John delivered the shirts to my house.

"I threw in five extra shirts—one in each size," he said.

The next day, we distributed the shirts, making sure each student got one in the size he or she had ordered.

"Do not take someone else's shirt, simply because the size you ordered feels too snug, or too loose,'" I warned.

"When are we going to wear them?" Becca, a first-period sixth grader asked.

"Good question, Becca. Would you mind giving everyone one of these, please?" I handed her a stack of handouts that read:

Starting the day after tomorrow and every Wednesday thereafter, all L2L students will be required to wear his or her L2L t-shirt to our class each and every week for the remainder of this school year. Those who do not will be refused admittance to our class and sent to the office that day, and every day thereafter, until such time as he or she wears his or her L2L t-shirt to our class.

"I chose Wednesdays, so we can all remind each other on Mondays ... and again on Tuesdays ... to wear our t-shirts on Wednesdays, because any of you who come to class that day not wearing it will get to explain to Mr. Callaghan or Mrs. Thomas why you are sitting in the front office," I said, after having Becca read the handout aloud after everyone had gotten one.

"How many of you believe I am serious about this? Raise your hands," I asked. Predictably, there were a couple of Doubting Thomases who did not raise their hands. I jotted down each of their names.

"Everyone, please take that handout home to your parents so they can also help remind you to wear your t-shirt on Wednesdays, and so they won't be surprised when you are sent out of class when you don't," I said. "As for those of you who didn't raise your hands because you apparently think I am kidding about this, I want you to take that handout home, get it signed by one of your parents, and bring it back to me ... *tomorrow*," I continued, as I held up my list of ne'er-do-wells, then looked directly at each of them.

That scenario repeated itself in similar manner in every class that day.

"Can I wear mine tomorrow?" Becca asked.

"Let's all wait until Wednesday for the big unveiling, this first time. Then you may wear it as often as you wish."

The very first Wednesday, one, two, or three kids in each class period—mostly boys—came to class without their L2L t-shirts.

"Everyone not wearing their L2L shirt, please go wait for me in the hallway. And take your backpacks and other belongings with you," I instructed in each class, as soon as the tardy bell rang.

Once the other students started working on that day's one-question quiz, I joined the scofflaws in the hallway. In every instance a half-hearted, "I forgot" was their excuse.

"Bummer. You were reminded yesterday ... and the day before. Yet, here we stand, me wearing my L2L shirt ... you not wearing yours," I replied. "And if you come to class tomorrow not wearing it, you'll be going right back to the office."

"But tomorrow is Thursday; not Wednesday," someone objected.

"Yes. It certainly is. And the next day is Friday, and you'll find yourself in the office again, if you don't wear your shirt tomorrow." There were non-verbal displays of displeasure, but no one spoke. "How many of you think I'm joking now? Raise your hands," I said. No one did.

"What are those kids going to learn by sitting in the

office?" one offender's mother asked when she called me to complain, after her daughter got home from school that afternoon.

"They'll learn to be responsible, and respectful," I said.

A couple of parents called to express dismay at my rigidity, and disappointment in their decision to enroll their child in my class. I respectfully reminded them that my class was an elective, which allowed them to have their child withdrawn and reassigned. None did.

That first Wednesday was tough. The second Wednesday was a little less so. But after that, the kids pretty much got the message. A few weeks later, however, three eighth-grade boys came to class that Wednesday wearing their football jerseys. I called them out into the hallway.

"We have a game this afternoon, and coach told us to wear our jerseys to school today," one young man informed me, rather curtly.

I walked over and opened the classroom door. "All three of you, look in that room and tell me if you see your coach in there," I said. They didn't move. "Go ahead, take a look," I insisted. They did. "I don't know what your coach told you, but I told you to wear your L2L shirt to my class today ... for this one period ... and that's what I expect," I explained. The three of them stood, arms folded, glaring at me defiantly. "I have an idea; come with me," I said, and headed for the gymnasium where I knew their coach was teaching a PE class.

"These three young men tell me they are going to do what you tell them to do in my class, rather than do what I tell them. So, starting right now, they can spend fifth period on Wednesdays with you ... while I count them absent and give them zeroes ... until such time as they reassess their priorities," I said. "And when they fail my class this quarter, they will be academically ineligible to play football," I reminded everyone, and walked away.

Right after school, before heading out to the football field for the game, the coach stopped by my classroom. "The boys and I had a heart-to-heart. That situation won't happen again," he said. I thanked him for his support.

The next morning, the mother of one of those boys called me before school started. "You obviously have no idea how important football is to those boys," she chided. To which I wanted to reply, "And you obviously have no idea how important my class is to me." But I refrained.

30

PARLEZ VOUS FRANCAIS?

ONCE I DISCOVERED HOW MUCH THE KIDS LOVED KNOWING stuff other people—especially adults—did not know, I decided to introduce them to a foreign language. It would perhaps have been more practical to teach them a little Spanish, but many of my students were Hispanic, and were already fluent in Español. I didn't want to exclude them, so I chose French.

Which Reminds Me: One day during an after-school faculty meeting, Mr.

Callaghan said to Cathy, one of our language arts teachers, "I want you to start working with the Hispanic students who don't speak English very well."

"Dan, you know I don't speak Spanish," Cathy exclaimed, sounding surprised and apprehensive.

"They already speak Spanish, Cathy; I want you to teach them to speak English."

When I told the kids we were going to learn to speak French, all I got were blank stares. They were not opposed. They simply were not optimistic.

"You already know at least one French word," I said. "What is that word?" I asked.

"Renaissance," someone in each class eventually offered, after some coaxing.

"What does it mean, in English?"

"Rebirth."

"Rebirth of what?"

"Art," Kassidy said, when I asked that question in third period.

"How do you spell it?"

"A...r...t" she instantly replied. I cocked my head and gave her "a look." She grinned. Everyone else snickered. "R...e...n...a...i...s...s...a...n...c...e," Kassidy added, rather amused by her wit. I must admit; it was pretty funny.

"But before you start learning a foreign language, you must first learn to spell *foreign*," I said. "So, who wants to go to the board and give it a shot?" They were not bashful about trying. There was fourrain ... and fourran ... and forran ... long before there was foreign. It took a while for everyone to leave out the persistent "u" and "a," and insert the reluctant "i" and "g." Maddie, a prolific reading sixth grader was the first to spell it correctly, right off the bat. And win a Tootsie Roll.

Wednesdays were designated "Je Parie Francais Day," and we began by learning to count to ten, then learning the days of the week, followed by learning the months of the year. Every day, I greeted each class with, "Bon jour. Comment allez-vous?" and taught them to respond with, "Tres bien, merci. Et toi?" Soon, the kids were entering other classes and greeting other teachers in French, prompting some of those teachers to good-naturedly accuse me of being a troublemaker.

HERDING CATS—LITERALLY

IT WAS EASTER WEEKEND. WE WERE ON SPRING BREAK. THAT Saturday morning, I went to a Home Depot near our house to purchase pine straw for mulching Gerry's flowerbeds.

"I need fifteen bales," I told the cashier in the garden equipment rental department. He took my money and gave me my change and receipt.

"They're in the truck trailer, out back. Would you mind going in there and getting the bales yourself? The trailer is unlocked," the clerk said. "I'm alone here, with this line of customers."

When I got out back, I climbed into the half-filled-with-straw trailer and started moving bales, two at a time, from the center of the trailer to the rear doorway. When I removed the fifth and sixth bales from the stack, I uncovered a squirming, squeaking ball of fur, but it was too dark to make out what I was looking at. I walked to the rear of the trailer and swung open the second of the double doors, to let in more light. When I got back to the noisy fuzz ball, I discovered three baby kittens, barely bigger than my thumb. I could easily hold all three in the palm of my hand.

Without a second thought, I found a small cardboard box by the dumpster, fetched a shop cloth from my truck, spread it on the bottom of the box, placed the kittens inside the box, placed the box on the seat of my truck, and finished loading my pine straw bales.

"Look what I've got," I said to Gerry when I walked up onto our back deck where she was busy planting impatiens. She turned, looked inside the box, then looked up at me like I was a crazy.

"What ... on ... earth?"

"Today's special at Home Depot: one free kitten with every five bales of pine straw," I joked, then told her the story of my discovery.

"We need to take them to a vet, right now. My sister-in-law, Kathy, has a dog and a cat; she'll have a vet recommendation. I'll give her a call," Gerry said.

Within an hour, we had the little critters at a nearby 24/7 veterinary clinic.

"These kittens—the two black ones are female, the grey one is male—are no more than three or four days old. They're malnourished and dehydrated, but we're trying to get some liquid into them," the vet said.

"What do I feed them? How do I feed them? When do I feed them?" I asked, totally out of my element.

"Goats milk will work, but if you're short on goats you can buy powdered formula from the PetSmart across the street; it comes with a tiny baby bottle. Mix the powder with boiling water until it dissolves, and feed it to them—not too hot, not too cold—every two hours, around the clock," the doc advised.

When we got home, we placed the little urchins on a bath towel inside a copier paper box and put them in my home office. It soon became obvious that the towel was a bad idea. We replaced it with newspaper.

After fumblingly feeding them for the first time, I set a timer to alert me every two hours to feed them again, all of which led me to a new appreciation for motherhood.

On Tuesday morning, I packed a kitten version of a diaper bag, placed the kittens snugly inside a plastic cat carrier borrowed from a neighbor, and carted them off to school so their feeding schedule could be maintained.

As soon as I got to school, I reported to Mr. Callaghan that I had kittens in my supply closet that would need feeding throughout the day but assured him it would not disrupt business as usual.

"How old are they?" he asked.

"I'm thinking eight to ten days, now."

"Have they opened their eyes yet?"

"They're trying."

"Let's go take a look."

"Are you feeding them every couple of hours?" Mr. Callaghan asked as he peered into the box.

"Like clockwork."

"What time do they need to be fed next?" he asked, as he held and lightly stroked the fur of each one, in turn.

"I'm going to feed them now, so after that, about 8:30."

"I'll come back and do that ... if the building's not on fire."

That is how I discovered Mr. Callaghan was a devout cat-person, with two kittens of his own at home.

Within minutes of Mr. Callaghan leaving my classroom, Ms. Adcock walked in.

"I hear you have some new babies," she beamed. I showed them to her. She gently picked up and petted each one too. "I'll want to come back and feed them, during my planning period," she offered. And she did. Almost every day.

I introduced the kittens to each of my classes that first day.

"Can we hold 'em?"

"Not yet."

As the age levels of my students increased throughout the day, from sixth to seventh to eighth graders, their levels of enthusiasm about helping feed the kittens decreased proportionally.

"What are their names?" was usually the first question.

"My wife named the black one with the tiny white spot under her chin Midnight ... the solid black one is April ... and the solid grey one's name is Sterling, like sterling silver."

As the kittens got bigger, they went from eating a fraction of a bottle of formula ... to a fourth ... to a half ... to a whole bottle. That is when I started mixing formula in a saucer with Fancy Feast. As they got more active, they graduated from their copier paper carton to a huge toilet paper box I got from Mr. Hunt, one of our custodians. Eventually I started giving them free reign of the classroom while I was at lunch.

On one occasion, as I sat chatting with colleagues at the

teachers' lunch table in the cafeteria, I was approached by a smallish sixth grader I had not yet had the privilege to teach.

"Mr. Massey," she said, after tapping me on the shoulder. "When we came past your classroom, there was cats running around everywhere," she calmly reported.

"You ... are ... kidding!" I replied.

"No, I ain't."

"Let's go take a look."

When she and I got to my classroom and peered through the long, narrow glass slot in the door, sure enough, "There was cats running around, everywhere."

"See!" she said, as if feeling validated.

"What's your name, young lady?" I asked, as I unlocked the door.

"Tina."

When we walked into the room, the kittens scurried toward us.

"You can pick them up, gently, if you want," I said to Tina when she gave me a pleaful look.

I transported the kittens back and forth between home and school every school day until they were old enough to wean. At ten weeks of age, I adopted them out. One of my students took Midnight, to replace her cat that had recently died. Gerry's sister-in-law, Kathy, that had recommended the vet, took April, but renamed her Rosie. And Kathy's friend, Kim, adopted Sterling.

LET THE GAMES BEGIN

WORD TO THE WISE FOR NEW TEACHERS: KIDS WANT TO BE entertained while being educated, so make learning a game; a competition. Kids who couldn't care less about a grade will scratch and claw to win a prize. But consolation prizes—participation trophies—accomplish nothing, except to undermine a winner's sense of accomplishment.

Looking Before Leaping

ONE OF THE HARDEST THINGS TO GET KIDS TO DO IS READ directions and follow instructions, as was always borne out by some version of the "Gotcha" quiz I administered to my students at the beginning of every school year.

"Before you begin this quiz, read *all* instructions at the top of the sheet," I would advise after distributing copies of the quiz.

Instructions;

1. Write your name in the upper left corner of your paper.
2. Write the number of this class period under your name.
3. Put today's date in the upper right corner of your paper.
4. Read *every* question before starting this quiz.
5. Once you have written your name in the upper left corner of your paper, turn your paper face down and put down your pencil.

Congratulations. You have just made a grade of 100 on this quiz.

In all likelihood, two, maybe three, students—almost always girls—would read the instructions and comply. By the time those few kids laid down their pencils as instructed, the majority had forged ahead and were already on question number three or four.

Once everyone had answered all questions, I had the kids exchange papers with the students at the table behind or beside them.

"Someone please read to us instruction number one," I would request. The kids that had complied with the instructions to start with were always eager to read them again, aloud, with puffed-out chest.

"And number two."

"Number three."

"Four."

"Five." Instruction number five being read out loud was always met with a mixture of surprise and embarrassment, followed by moans and groans of righteous indignation at having been "tricked."

"Bummer."

"It's not fair!"

"Please write the grade—either 100 or zero—at the top of the paper, and pass them to the center aisle," I would instruct, inciting a din of unintelligible mumbles and grumbles as grades were harshly scribed onto papers and papers were dramatically slapped into stacks at the ends of each table.

I always recorded the grades of the students who made a 100; it helped their end-of-quarter grade averages. Unbeknown to the kids who did not follow instructions, however, I never recorded their zeroes, so their end-of-quarter grade averages were not negatively impacted.

PB&J ... Or ... J&PB?

TO IMPRESS UPON MY STUDENTS THE IMPORTANCE OF ADEQUATE and accurate instructions, and to encourage them to *read* instructions before plowing ahead with any task, I had my kids, working in teams of two, *write* step-by-step directions for one of the most mundane of mundane undertakings— making a peanut butter and jelly sandwich.

"You have the remainder of this class period and all of tomorrow's to finish this assignment. Then, using your own instructions, each team will, in turn, attempt to make a sandwich. I will furnish the fixings. If you do so, without omitting a step, you will get to eat your tasty sandwich in class. I will also provide milk to wash it down," I informed each class. If someone asked, "What kind of milk, regular or chocolate?" I would say, "Buttermilk."

Making a sandwich, Easy peasy, huh? Not so much.

"You've spent two class periods working on your list of instructions. Today I want you to work with your teammate in performing a step-by-step dry run, imagining you're making a sandwich."

"What should we do when we finish that?" Dominick asked in second period, apparently expecting to breeze through the practice exercise.

"Imagine eating it," I said. Sometimes the kids didn't get my sense of humor. That was one of those times.

On day four of the PB&J project, I brought to class loaves of bread, big jars of jelly—grape and strawberry—and giant containers of peanut butter—smooth and crunchy, all in the knick of time. The kids were weary of writing, and anxious to eat.

"Who wants to go first?"

Without fail, an over-zealous team would respond by jumping up and down,

waving their hands in the air, clamoring, "Ooo ... Ooo ... us ... us ... let us!" reminiscent of Arnold Horshack on the TV sitcom *Welcome Back Kotter.*

Standing in front of the class, ingredients and utensils arrayed on a table in front

of them, the first team of volunteers would confidently set

about creating a JIF and Smuckers snack as their eager-to-find-fault classmates sat in judgment.

"Step #1: Remove bread from package."

"Ha ha! You didn't say, 'Open the package,' first."

"And you didn't say 'Remove the twist-tie.'"

"And you didn't say how many slices of bread to remove from the package!"

"And you didn't say what kind of bread!"

Criticism of classmates in middle school could be, and usually was, endless.

"Our bread didn't have a twist-tie."

"Everybody knows you use *two* slices of bread."

Making excuses was also commonplace.

"Okay. Okay. Okay. Let's not get carried away," I would interject, after letting them banter for a short while.

Dejected and deprived of PB&J, team one would take their seats, only to be replaced in the hot seat by team two.

Rinse and repeat.

Middle-schoolers would much rather catch someone else —especially teachers—

being wrong than to be right themselves—about anything. My students particularly relished me making a mistake. "I thought I was wrong once, but I was mistaken," was always my retort to their allegations of a misstep.

"Now seems like a good time for everyone to review their instructions,

and make sure you won't wind up removing peanut butter from its jar without taking off the lid ... or spreading jelly on bread without benefit of a knife," I would advise at the end of their first attempts at sandwich construction.

The following day, and the day after that, and the day after that, for however long

it took, we would attempt to make sandwiches, until every team had successfully done so. And eaten a PB&J sandwich. And made a grade of 100. A lesser grade was not possible.

In the end, each team wound up with a forty- or fifty-step set of instructions, starting out as tediously detailed as:

1. Pick up loaf of bread
2. Remove tie-wrap
3. Place tie-wrap on table
4. Open bread package
5. Reach inside package
6. Remove two slices of bread
7. Place bread on a saucer or napkin
8. Close the package
9. Pick up tie-wrap
10. Replace tie-wrap
11. Lay loaf of bread on table
12. Pick up jar of peanut butter
13. Yadda
14. Yadda
15. Yadda

"But we're only making a stupid sandwich," someone would always complain.

"Suppose you were preparing the space shuttle for launch?"

"Is that what happened to the Challenger? Someone didn't follow the directions?"

"Hmm. Something to think about. Huh?"

Going The Extra Mile: "There are five different colors of tie-wraps on bread packages—blue, green, red, white, yellow—and the color tells you what day of the week that loaf of bread was baked. I looked it up online," Jada informed our class one day. Who knew?

Misspelling And Misplacing Mississippi

M - I - CROOKED LETTER - CROOKED LETTER - I - CROOKED letter - crooked letter - i - humpback - humpback - i. That is how we were taught to correctly spell Mississippi when I was in third grade, or thereabout.

We were discussing how odd it seemed to us that some famous artists—Monet, Rembrandt, Klee, Da Vinci, Picasso—spoke different languages—French, Dutch, German, Italian, Spanish—despite living only a few hundred miles from each other.

"It would be as if our family and friends in Richmond spoke Virginian, while we all spoke North Carolinian," I suggested. "What other languages might our family and friends from other neighboring states speak?" No one responded. I wrote Virginia on the board. "What are the other four states that share a border with North Carolina?" I prompted.

"South Carolina."

"Write it on the board," I said, offering a dry-erase marker.

After some heavy hinting, and discounting the suggestion that Florida was a bordering neighbor, our list had grown to include Georgia and Tennessee.

"One more; what is it?" I coaxed.

"Paris," someone seriously offered, and no one else objected.

Oh my God.

That weekend, I went to the Teach Me Store and bought eight large, 50-piece jigsaw puzzles. Each of our fifty US states were a puzzle piece. The following week I announced a new class contest.

"On Wednesdays, starting today, working as teams of four with your tablemates, we are going to learn the geographic locations and correct spellings of our fifty states," I announced, as I placed a puzzle box and a black permanent marker on each table. There were smiles. And there were frowns.

"Using the markers, someone please write the color of your table on the bottom of your puzzle box," I instructed. "Why? Because I want each table to always use the same box. Why? So if you are careless and lose a puzzle piece, you will always be the ones who have to work without it. Why write it on the bottom? Because I don't want you to write it over the map pictured on the lid. Any questions?"

There were mad scrabbles at each table as everyone grappled for the marker.

"Whoa! Hold your horses; here comes the best part—I want you to use the French word for the color of your tables," I added. "Now, do you have questions?" Hands flew up all over the room.

"Will those of you who successfully wrestled the markers away from your tablemates in that little melee please come stand by the flipchart? Do not write on the dry-erase board with those permanent markers." I waited as the eight of them congregated.

"Red, in French, is rouge ... r-o-u-g-e. Please write that on the flipchart, then take your seat."

We went through that routine for each of the eight applicable colors: red, blue, yellow, purple, green, orange, black, white—rouge, bleu, jaune, violet, vert, orange, noir, blanc.

"Those of you with the markers, please hand them to someone else at your table," I said, once everyone was re-seated. "And those of you who get the markers, please write the color of your table on the bottom of your puzzle box, in Francias, sil vous plait."

Once that undertaking was done, before we could carry on, we had a brief discussion about, "Why do the French misspell blue?" and "Why don't they have their own word for orange?"

"Now take a moment to *carefully* pour the puzzle pieces onto your tables and ..."

"You didn't say, 'Open the box,' before you said, 'Pour the puzzle pieces out,'" Cory pointed out, goading me about my not-so-flawless instructions.

"Cory, you ever hear the expression, 'Cutting off your nose to spite your face?'" He had not. No one had. So I continued, "... pour the puzzle pieces onto your tables and place the box aside, face down, so you can't see the map pictured on the front. Then turn the puzzle pieces face up ... keeping all fifty states on your tables ... *please*." I gave them a couple of minutes. "Now, find the puzzle piece for Hawaii, and place it in the center of your table." They did. "Someone name a state that borders Hawaii, please." No response, only blank expressions. I waited.

"Mr. Massey, ain't no states that border Hawaii ... it's an island ... in the middle of the ocean," Jasmine finally said, as if scolding me. I almost asked, "Which ocean?" but left well enough alone.

"Hmm. In that case, find and place North Carolina in the center of your tables, then locate the five states we identified last week as our bordering neighbors. When you have done that, raise your hands."

Each time someone raised their hand, I walked over and checked for accuracy. If all was good to go, everyone at that table got a bite-size Tootsie Roll.

"Now ... when I say 'Go' ... I want you to place those five states in their correct geographic positions around North Carolina; the first team to correctly do so will get Tootsie Pops." (One might suspect the NC Association of Dentists was sponsoring my class.) "On your mark ... are ... you ... ready? Go!"

Completion of that task took longer than it should have, but not nearly as long as it would have a week earlier.

"Okay, now, using the map photo on your puzzles' box top as a guide, identify and find the puzzle pieces for the ten states that surround and border Virginia, West Virginia, Tennessee, Georgia, and South Carolina. You have five minutes."

After about three minutes, the initial flurries of activity slowed to a tedious search among the loose puzzle pieces. Finally, someone raised their hand and declared, "Mr. Massey, we can only find nine states that do that."

"Exactly. Go get Tootsie Pops for you and your teammates."

"Not fair. You tricked us," someone else complained.

"Teaching is always tricky," I said. "Besides, as my grandma once said to me when I griped that having to pick fifty pounds of cotton on Saturday mornings before being allowed to go to the afternoon matinee movie wasn't *fair*— 'The Fair is where your daddy takes you young'uns in October. That's got nothing to do with pickin' cotton.'"

I considered pointing out that my grandma knew all fifty states, where they were located, and how to spell them correctly, despite her meager eighth-grade education, but thought better of it. It might encourage some of them to set their sights on dropping out of school at age fourteen.

Eventually we had listed Maryland, Kentucky, Ohio, Pennsylvania, Mississippi, Alabama, Arkansas, Missouri, and Florida on the board.

We practiced until each team could correctly assemble the puzzle pieces for the five states that border North Carolina and the nine states that border those five. Then we moved out from there, and out from there, until we had covered all fifty states.

The advantage I had in L2L over my colleagues who taught core subjects—math, science, language arts, and social studies—was that I didn't have pacing guides to follow. I didn't have to be on such and such a page in a textbook by such and such a date. They did. I got to *teach* material before moving on. They did not have that latitude. They had to *cover* the material, as best they could, in the time allotted, then move on, regardless.

Philosophical question: Is it better that kids learn all fifty states in our country before moving on to learn all nine planets in our solar system (if you still count Pluto, which the kids tend to do) or is it preferable to learn thirty-seven of the fifty states by Friday, before moving on to learn six of the nine planets by the following Wednesday, before moving on to learn five of the seven continents by the next Monday? Just sayin'.

"Are we going to have a quiz on this?" someone finally asked; Joshell, I think.

"Kind of. I'm going to divide the class into two groups—the primary color tables plus the white table working together, and the secondary color tables plus the black table working together—to write your own rap song that mentions all fifty states." (I knew they knew by heart the lyrics to practically every song they had ever heard—the good, the bad, and yes, the ugly.)

I waited a moment for the hubbub of excitement to die down.

"Then, both groups will perform your songs in the cafeteria, during lunchtime, in front of the cafeteria crowd. That will be your quiz."

"When?"

"Two weeks from today."

"How will you decide what our grade is from them listening to us sing?"

"I'll use my applause meters," I said as I pointed to my ears.

Calculated Risk

AFTER WAITING IN A SHORT LINE AT THE MOVIE BOX OFFICE, Gerry and I purchased tickets to see *The King's Speech*, a newly released, highly acclaimed movie about King George VI's unexpected ascendance to the British throne when his older brother Edward VIII abdicated to marry an American commoner.

As soon as our tickets were taken, Gerry headed straight for the theater to find a couple of decent seats, while I queued-up in one of three lines at the concessions stand. After five minutes of snails-paced progress, I stepped out of line to see what was holding things up.

"The computerized registers are offline; every transaction is being processed manually," an equally impatient moviegoer ahead of me in line explained.

"May I help you?" a teen-looking cashier—Charlene, according to her plastic name badge—asked when I finally reached the front of the line. She was obviously a bit stressed.

"I'd like one large bucket of popcorn, no butter ... a box of Raisinets ... and a large Diet Coke, light on ice, please."

Charlene put ice in a cup, drew the fountain Diet Coke, sat it on the counter in front of me, removed the Raisinets from the candy showcase and placed them beside the Coke, while a concessions co-worker filled a bucket with freshly popped corn and sat it beside the Coke and candy. I held out a twenty-dollar bill, but Charlene ignored it. She was busy turning in circles, frantically looking around the cash register area beside her and the counter surface behind her. "Who took my calculator?" she shouted, sounding both miffed and panicked. No one fessed up.

"My total is $17.50—$7.50 plus $4.50 plus $5.50—so you

owe me $2.50, in change," I said. Charlotte took my money, looked at me as if bewildered, then looked over at her mid-twenties-looking supervisor. He took out his own calculator, tallied my tab, and gave her a confirming nod. She gave me two one-dollar bills and two quarters, and wished me an enjoyable movie. I walked away, hoping she would soon find her calculator.

"May I please have a medium and a large popcorn, a medium Coke and a small Sprite, a box of Sno-Caps, and a package of licorice Twizzlers, please," the guy behind me was saying to Charlene as I was gathering my goodies and getting a few napkins.

"Oh my God. Good luck with that, buddy," I thought as I walked away.

"Why did that take you so long?" Gerry asked as I settled into the seat beside her.

"It didn't take *me* long. But Charlene struggled mightily."

"Who?"

That experience set me to wondering about how and why that young woman and her slightly older supervisor were so lacking in simple addition and subtraction skills, and were so inept at something as basic but critical as making change?

The next day—Saturday—I purchased eight pint-size faux-Tupperware containers and eight disposable aluminum foil pie tins from Kmart. On Monday afternoon, on my way home from school, I stopped at my bank and obtained enough change to put two half-dollars, four quarters, ten dimes, twenty nickels, and a hundred pennies into each of those containers. That night, using a permanent marker, I labeled each container the color of a classroom table—red, yellow, blue, orange, purple, green, black, or white. I wanted the kids to feel some sense of ownership responsibility for safeguarding *their* container of coins.

"What's this for?" Prinzess asked as I placed a container of coins on each table, according to color.

"If I gave you a dollar to pay for something...

"Don't open that, until I ask you to, please," I said to someone else who was about to.

"—to pay for something that cost seventy-eight cents, how much change would you give me back?" I asked Prinzess. She did not answer. "Seventy-eight cents from a dollar; how much change? Anybody?" I persisted as I looked from table to table, awaiting a response.

"What did you buy?" someone asked, trying to change the subject, I assumed.

"What is something that might cost seventy-eight cents? You tell me." I waited. They squirmed.

"Your change is twenty-two cents—two pennies and two dimes," Cheyenne said. She knew the answer all along, but she and I had agreed she would not blurt out answers to questions I asked in class until other kids had a chance. The other kids respected rather than resented Cheyenne because she was never arrogant. But she was often bored.

"Exactly. And that's what these coins are for ... we're all going to learn to do that ... to make change using our heads, not calculators."

"Why?" someone asked. I knew that was coming, but I ignored it and moved on.

There was a lot of shaking and rattling of coin containers and giggling taking place, as I passed out the foil pie plates.

I walked to the front of the classroom, leaned against the edge of my desk, and waited. In a moment the kids fell silent when they realized I was silent. And watching.

"Okay, here we go again; I owe you sixty-seven cents. I give you a dollar. How much change do I get?" No immediate reply. "Is it easier to add numbers in your head, or subtract them?"

"Add!" everyone decisively shouted.

"In that case, let's add. How many cents in a dollar?"

"One hundred."

"So, sixty-seven plus three pennies is seventy ... seventy plus three dimes is eighty ... ninety ... one hundred. You owe me three pennies and three dimes, which totals ... how much?"

"Thirty-three cents!" two students replied, one sounding more certain than the other.

"Ah! It's as simple as that. Now, pour the coins from your containers into the pie plates. Then spread the coins around so you can more easily see them. But do it care ... ful ... ly. We don't want coins all over the floor, no matter how happy that would make Mr. Hunt when he sweeps up at lunchtime."

For the remainder of that day, and one day each week for the remainder of that quarter, we engaged in making-change exercises.

"When I shout out an amount and say 'GO,' I want you, as teams, to count out that amount of change ... using the *least* number of coins possible ... and place them on your tables. When you have done so, raise your hands. First team to be correct gets Tootsie Rolls."

Eventually, the kids stopped eating their candy as soon as they earned it, and the biggest pile of Tootsie Rolls at the end of class became their trophy. I am quite certain unleashing a mob of sugar-addled teens upon my fellow teachers practically every day was not the most popular thing I ever did.

"For instance, if I shout out twenty-two cents, you could give me twenty-two pennies ... or two pennies and four nickels... or two pennies and two dimes. But which of those combinations would be correct; would be the least number of coins?"

"The last one!"

"Correct. Good. So, let's get started: thirty-seven cents ... GO!"

The more we practiced, the more complicated I made the challenge. Pretty soon I threw multiplication into the equation.

"I buy a Coke for seventy-five cents and a bag of chips for forty-five cents and I give you two one-dollar bills. How much do I owe you ... *after* you add ten percent sales tax? And how much change do I get back, using the least number of coins?" Everyone waited at the ready for me to say "GO." "Who remembers the easiest way to figure ten percent of any number?" I asked. (Sales tax was actually seven percent, but, baby steps.)

"Move the decimal one place to the left," a bunch of kids shouted back.

"Correctamundo."

"Huh?"

"Never mind. You obviously don't know about Fonzie," I said, before shouting, "GO!"

In way less than a minute—a fraction of the time it would have taken a few weeks earlier—hands started popping up.

"Green table, you were first. How much?"

"You owe us $1.20 plus twelve cents tax ... that's $1.32 ... so your change is sixty-eight cents ... or a half-dollar, a dime, a nickel, and three pennies."

"Tootsie Rolls for the green table!"

We had managed to disguise learning as *winning*.

A Sign Of The Times

I DON'T KNOW WHEN IT HAPPENED, BUT SOMEWHERE ALONG THE way before I started teaching, the public-school system's powers that be decided teaching the "times tables" was no longer a worthwhile endeavor. Kids were being taught to work math problems without any understanding of how or why the system of math worked. The answer became more important than the solution. That became dismayingly obvious when trying to get my students to figure and add a tax or subtract a discount during our making-change exercises.

Out of curiosity one day, as soon as the kids in my first-period class settled into their seats, I asked, "How much is five times nine?"

"Can we use a calculator?" someone asked, almost before the last word of the question crossed my lips. How many times had I heard that?

"Only the one between your ears," I replied. How many times had I said that?

There was no further response, except for befuddled looks. I had mistakenly assumed the 5-times table would be the easiest for them.

"How about two times nine?" No response. After waiting a long moment, I looked over at Cheyenne, and nodded.

"It's eighteen," she softly said. "and five times nine is forty-five," she added. I walked over, quietly handed her a Tootsie Pop, and gave her an "Atta girl" pat on the shoulder. It had previously become obvious that I needed to start awarding candy to the first two teams to correctly answer a question or accurately solve a problem. Otherwise, if I only rewarded the first team to do so, Cheyenne would always win. But if I required her to hold back, she would rarely ever win.

That night I hand wrote worksheets for the 2-times table through the 12-times table on copier paper using a black Flair felt-tip pen to make them big and bold. I knew the kids would simply memorize the answers if I wrote the problems in numerical order—2 x 2 = ... 2 x 3 = ... 2 x 4 = ... etc.—so I wrote them out of sequence—2 x 7 = ... 2 x 12 = ... 2 x 5 = ... etc.

The following day, as soon as I finished taking roll, I had the captains of each class pass out two copies of the 3-times table worksheet to each table. "Place them face down on the tables," I instructed the captains. "Don't turn those over until I tell you to, and make sure your team has a sharpened pencil," I instructed the class. My directions were met with "Now what?" stares. They never knew what to expect when I introduced one of my brainchild activities.

"Working in teams of two ... you and the person sitting beside you ... please complete, as quickly but accurately as possible, the worksheet lying in front of you," I said. Suspecting they were going to be timed, anxious hands inched their way toward the worksheets. "Not until I tell you to start," I warned, letting them fidget for a moment. Sometimes at moments like that, I would taunt them a bit to lighten the mood. "Ready" ... "Set" ... I would say, dragging out the start command before suddenly blurting out, "Good luck." As soon as they heard "Good..." they were off to the races. "Eh, eh, eh ... I did not say go. Put 'em back." Half of them were amused by that. Half of them were annoyed. But that tidbit of goofing around made learning the times tables more like fun, less like schoolwork.

When I finally said, "GO," for real, they snatched up the papers and flipped them face-up in one blurred motion. Then, seeing what they had in their hands, they froze, as if someone had hit their *pause* buttons. They stared at the paper, then slowly looked up at me. "You're wasting time," I calmly said.

It took Cheyenne and Caitlyn thirty seconds to complete the worksheet with all correct answers. The next fastest team took more than a minute, counting on their fingers. They had one incorrect answer.

Each of my classes went through that exercise that day, with similar results. The exception was Will, from the sixth-grade boys class. He turned out to be as quick and accurate as Cheyenne. Beyond that, as for everyone else, *oh brother!*

We went through that exercise one class period a week, for four weeks. We went through each of the times tables many times.

"Today, I am going to pass around a sign-up sheet for

voluntary participation in a tournament we..." I started to announce on Wednesday of the fifth week.

"What multiplication tournament?" I was anxiously asked.

"The one I was in the midst of telling you about."

There were some to-be expected moans and groans, but quite a bit of excited buzz as well. Initially, about half the students in each class signed up.

"Posted on the wall beside the supply closet are tournament brackets for each class period, like the ones used for March Madness," I said and pointed toward the brackets. "Using these sign-up sheets, we will fill out those brackets, and every Wednesday we will have competitions, only this time you'll compete as individuals, not as teams," I explained. More moans and groans. "Once the winner of each class is determined, we will create playoff brackets. In the first playoff round, our first-period winner will take on our second-period winner ... our third-period winner will challenge our fourth-period winner ... and fifth period will oppose sixth period."

"Maybe we could call our tournament *Multiplication Madness*," someone proudly shouted out.

"That's not an all-bad suggestion," I admitted.

"What do the winners win?"

"Hold your horses, Kimosabe. Once a winner is determined for each grade level, the sixth-grade winner will take on the seventh-grade winner. Then that winner will compete against the eighth-grade winner in the championship game."

Oddly enough, the sixth graders were excited about their prospects of "beating" the upper-level champs. They knew two of their own, Cheyenne and Will, had by far been the fastest participants in our practice rounds.

"Then will the winners have won something?"

"No, but they will have earned something," I said. "Debra Morgan, a news anchor for WRAL-TV, an acquaintance of my wife and I, has kindly agreed to give the two top finishers from each class a guided tour of the TV station, including being allowed to remain in the studio while she and Gerald Owens broadcast the evening news, live," I explained. The kids who had signed up for the tournament perked up. "I am also going to draw two names from each class so other participants in the tournament are rewarded for their hard work, too," I said. That added to the smile count.

"How many of you watch the evening news?" I asked. A few hands went up.

"The news is boring," several kids mumbled. But there were also a lot of positive comments.

"I watch the news with my parents, while we eat dinner."

"I watch the weather with my grandma. She thinks Greg Fishel is funny."

"My dad and I watch sports with Tom Suiter, or sometimes with Jeff Gravley. My dad said Jeff Gravley went to school here in Oxford, and graduated from J.F. Webb High School."

"He certainly did," I confirmed. "Mr. Gravley and I once spoke about his fond memories of time spent at Webb. He's a very proud graduate."

I let the kids murmur excitedly about the WRAL trip for a few moments before continuing. "But wait, there's more," I exclaimed, mimicking Ron Popeil on those cheesy late-night

Ronco TV commercials. "On our way home from our TV station tour, we're going to stop at Amedeo's, a famous Italian restaurant in Raleigh, for an all-you-can-eat spaghetti dinner, paid for with money left over from your last fundraiser," I announced. A shot at free food always elevated the kids' level of enthusiasm. That fact was not lost on me.

"Can I have pizza, instead of spaghetti? I like pizza better," Brianna, one of my seventh graders, asked.

"Is there anything else I can do to please your picky palette?" I asked, facetiously.

"You gotta win first ... or get your name picked in the drawing," someone chimed in.

"Oh ... I'm gonna win ... believe it," Brianna boasted. No one doubted her.

"Now that you all know what's in it for you ... other than a chance to demonstrate your abundance of brilliance ... I'm going to pass the sign-up sheet around again, in case there are some changes of heart about participating," I explained.

On the second go-round, there were two or three add-ons to the sheet in each class. Later, over the next couple of days, several kids approached me with requests to withdraw. "Sorry. This is like the army—you sign on the dotted line, you report for duty," I replied, losing a vote for "favorite teacher," each time.

In each round of head-to-head tournament competition, two contestants sat at side-by-side tables, with pencils anxiously at the ready. Class captains drew a slip of paper upon which a number between two and twelve had been written. That number determined which times table those two students were about to tackle. The captain handed me two blank copies of the selected worksheet and I placed a copy in front of each competitor, face down.

"As soon as you complete this worksheet, place it face down onto the table and place your pencil on top of it." That's what I told the competitors. What they apparently heard was, "As soon as you complete this worksheet, slap your paper face down onto the table as loudly as possible, and bang your pencil down on top of it as hard as you can."

When I gave the "GO" command, worksheets were grabbed and flipped, and pencils flew as answers were furiously scribbled.

The instant each competitor finished and flipped his or her paper face down, a designated stopwatch keeper recorded that student's elapsed time on the board. When both competitors were finished and their times recorded, two other students checked both worksheets for errors. Five seconds were added to a competitor's total time for each incorrect answer. Then a winner—the one with the lowest total time after adjustments were made—was declared. That student got to go to the supply closet door and write his or her name on the next-round bracket, while the other students applauded; half of them out of genuine appreciation for a job well done; the other half as an excuse to make noise in class.

After four weeks of every-Wednesday tournament competition, the hoopla was over, and Will—having beaten Cheyenne by two seconds on the 11-times table worksheet in the championship round—was the overall champion of "Multiplication Madness."

Fifteen Seconds Of Fame

UPON OUR ARRIVAL AT WRAL ON THE EVENING OF OUR VISIT, as we were walking from the bus parking lot toward the studio lobby, Sky 5 was departing the roof-top helipad. As the high-pitch whine of the engine got louder and louder and the main rotor blades spun-up faster and faster, the pilot was smiling and waving to the kids. When it lifted off, it hovered briefly, then banked left and swooped away as the prop-wash blew hats and caps all over the courtyard. Some flew into the fountain, but none of that stopped that experience from being the thrill of the trip. I am quite certain more than one student made on-the-spot career decisions to become helicopter pilots.

Debra Morgan met us in the lobby and was most gracious in answering a flurry of questions from the kids. Several about the helicopter, the first being, "Have you ever ridden in it?"

"Yes. Often. Too often, for my liking," Debra admitted.

"What is something exciting that has happened to you as a TV reporter?" Katy—pronounced *kah-tee*—asked Debra.

"Well," Debra replied, without a second's hesitation, "going to a man's house to interview him and having him shoot at me and my cameraman was pretty exciting." Debra laughed. The kids got wide-eyed. I am quite certain more than one of them made on-the-spot decisions *not* to become TV news reporters.

When the six o'clock news was about to start, Gerald Owens joined Debra in the studio. Debra introduced Gerald to the kids, asked them to be as quiet as possible so as not to be heard on the air, then excused herself and took her seat beside Gerald at the news desk. When it was time for the weather segment of the broadcast, Mike Maze joined Debra and Gerald. The kids were disappointed it was not Greg Fishel. Sorry Mike. But they were soon pleased when home-town boy Jeff Gravley arrived on set to report sports news.

When the broadcast ended, Jeff walked over and chatted with the kids briefly. "My sister still works as a hair stylist in a beauty parlor in Oxford," he told them.

Debra spent more than an hour physically walking us through the vast WRAL complex, and verbally walking us through the technically intricate process of television produc-tion and broadcasting. The kids' favorite aspect of the tour was being allowed to stand, one at a time, in front of the big green weather-set chroma key wall, and, for about fifteen seconds each, watch themselves on the monitor as a control booth technician made any parts of their bodies that were clothed in green become transparent.

"You can see right through me," Katy exclaimed. If any of them did, I knew Katy would be the one most likely to someday become an on-air TV personality.

For four consecutive years after that visit, Debra hosted my students on similar tours, each time whetting the interest of some of them to consider careers in broadcast journalism. Or, as Quentin said on our first visit, "I'd rather be the cameraman."

Later at Amedeo's, while waiting to be seated, the kids—even the UNC and Duke diehards—enjoyed perusing the NC State Wolfpack football and basketball memorabilia displayed on the walls of the restaurant.

"I didn't know State won the national basketball championship," Trevon, one of my seventh graders, said, much to his surprise, and chagrin, I believe.

"Yep. Twice—1974 and 1983," I gloated. "In '73 and '74, when David Thompson played at State, their combined record was 57-1."

"Who's David Thompson?" Trevon innocently asked.

"Oh ... my ... God," I thought. "Who's Michael Jordan?" I wanted to ask. But didn't.

"I wasn't even born then," Marcus piped up. "I don't think my daddy was even born then."

Kids have no concept of time. I was in the Vietnam War, which is to them indistinguishable from the Civil War.

"How's that pizza you worked so hard to earn?" I asked Brianna, as the other kids ate spaghetti like they had not eaten in a week.

"Mr. Massey, this is the biggest pizza, ever. I can't eat any more."

"Well, we can't leave until you eat it all," I said, sounding as serious as a heart attack, before asking a waitress for a to-go box.

33

WELCOME TO WALMART

Toward the end of our efforts to learn the multiplication tables, I mentioned that monitoring stock market values was a practical use of mental math skills. It took a minute before I realized my students were associating my reference to stock market to mean the fenced-in facility out on Highway 15 where livestock was once bought and sold. Despite our ensuing discussion about the iconic trappings of Wall Street—daily ringing of the opening bell, chaotic shouting of stock orders, slowly crawling electronic tote board—we kind of wound up back on the subject of livestock—the famous bronze bull sculpture located at the intersection of Broadway and Morris Street in Lower Manhattan's Financial District.

"Tomorrow, I would like as many of you as possible to bring in one dollar, so ask your parents tonight, please," I announced to each class the following Wednesday. "Tell them we're going to buy one share of Walmart stock. And when we do, we'll all own a small piece of the Walmart Corporation ... not just one store," I explained. That's when it dawned on me that our newly built local Walmart store was located directly across Highway 15 from the long-standing livestock market.

"Will we be rich?" someone asked, in all sincerity.

"No, but we won't be broke, either," I said, as I retrieved from my briefcase the financial section of that day's edition of the *News & Observer* newspaper. I had made sixteen copies of the New York Stock Exchange stock values chart—two copies for each table.

"Walmart is listed on this chart as WMT. Tootsie Rolls for the first team of two—you and your tablemate—who finds it on this chart and figures out what a share of Walmart stock is worth today."

They found the listing fairly quickly but needed some assistance in deciphering the numbers.

"So, how much is one share of WMT stock worth this morning?" I asked.

"Seventy dollars and ... and ... twenty-nine cents," someone offered with a twinge of uncertainty.

"Right. And how much was it worth yesterday? That's listed too, on the same chart."

"Uh ... sixty-nine dollars ... eighty-one cents."

"So, is it worth more or less today than yesterday? You don't need a chart for that."

"More."

"How much more; it tells you, right on that chart."

"Forty-eight cents."

"That's not very much," Lizeth commented.

"It would be, if we owned a thousand shares," I pointed out. "In fact, how much is one thousand times forty-eight cents?" No immediate response. I looked over at Cheyenne.

"Four hundred eighty dollars," she said.

"How did you figure that, without a cal ... cu ... la ...tor?" I asked, drawing it out to tease them about their over-reliance.

"I moved the decimal three places to the right; once for each zero in thousand." That is what I meant by "understanding the *system* of math."

"Bingo!"

A similar version of that scenario played out in all six of my L2L classes that day.

The following day I collected all the dollar bills the kids had brought in. There were more than I expected, and several promises to "bring one after payday."

A week later, in first period, I let the class decide who among them would assist me in buying our one share of Walmart stock online, using the computer on my desk. They chose Bree. We charged it to my Visa card.

Several weeks later I received our stock certificate, addressed to me at our school. When class started that next Wednesday, I asked Bree, since she had helped me buy it online, to open the envelope in front of the class. The certificate was big, with blue print on crisp, crinkly white paper. We passed it around in every class period, so the kids could see and feel it.

"It only has your name on it," someone quickly pointed out in almost every class.

"That's the way it works; not enough room for everyone's

names. So, I am your trustee, charged with protecting your investment," I explained.

"Why can't I be trustee?" Jazmine (not to be confused with Jasmine) wanted to know.

"You can. But we'll need to use your credit card to make the purchase. Do you have it with you?" I asked. End of discussion.

Within a week of receiving our stock certificate, it was matted and framed, and hung on the wall beside our classroom door.

Every Wednesday started with in-class reviews of that day's NYSE chart, after which the two-person teams plotted line graphs on quadrille paper depicting the current value of a share of Walmart stock; graphs they were required to maintain for quarterly grades. Practically everything we did in L2L classes, we did as teams of two or groups of four, which at times proved to be a bit of a sticky wicket. "Why can't I do my own graph?" was a common question, at first. "She won't do her part!" or "He's making me do all the work," were common complaints.

"You are in teams for a reason, not for torment," I assured them. "Fact is, you will remember none of what you pretend to read. You will retain only half of what I tell you, provided you're even listening. But you will never forget anything you discuss with your teammate, group-mates, or classmates, especially if you disagree and respectfully argue about, and most especially if you lose the argument," I explained.

I once made joking reference to our "Walmart windfall," then explained the meaning of that term—windfall. From then on, the kids took to calling our stock market study time "Windfall Wednesdays."

In a lunchtime conversation with Mr. Quay, a sixth-grade social studies teacher, he mentioned his students, many of whom were also my students, were learning about Russia, including its monetary system, and a tiny light bulb flashed on in the back of my mind.

The following week I began requiring my students to start plotting and maintaining two updated line graphs—one reflecting the value of Walmart in US dollars, and the other in Russian rubles. The first day we did that, we spent an entire class period practicing the dollars-to-rubles exchange rate conversion process, without benefit of calculators—an affront to their Eighth Amendment protection against cruel and unusual punishment, to hear the kids tell it. Apparently, any exercise that involves long division is a clear violation of the Geneva Convention Accords. Who knew?

Nonetheless we persevered, and after a few weeks, we compared the two graphs to each other. One at a time, I had each team take their two graphs to the light-table and overlay them. I wanted them to see that even though the dollars versus rubles numbers were different, the trend of the plot lines were exactly the same.

"When you own stock, you should pay less attention to its short-term daily price—the dots—and focus more on its long-term direction of value—the line," I explained, in a feeble attempt to sound like Warren Buffet

Now, over a decade later, our Walmart stock certificate hangs in my home office. As of the date of this writing, it has a market value of $105.77 or 5,980 rubles—an increase of

51.5 percent since date of purchase. Too bad we didn't buy those 1,000 shares we talked about in class back then.

Every January I receive in the mail from Walmart a notification of gain or loss in value of our single share of its stock, which I dutifully report to the IRS, no later than April 15.

34

YOUR GUESS IS AS GOOD AS MINE

ONE AFTERNOON WHEN MY FOURTH-PERIOD CLASS OF SEVENTH graders was filtering into my classroom after lunch, our custodian, Mr. Hunt, was still sweeping our floor.

"Sorry to be in the way, but I had to wait a spell before taking out the trash; it was raining cats and dogs outside," he explained.

"Why do old folks say stuff like that? It's dumb. It can't rain cats and dogs," one of the kids rather brusquely asked as soon as Mr. Hunt left the room.

"It's an idiom, meant to emphasize a point," I explained. "Mr. Hunt was emphasizing how ridiculously hard it was raining."

"My grandma says that, too; about raining cats and dogs," someone else offered.

"Yeah. Cause she's old," the first student fired back.

"My daddy says, 'A penny saved is a penny earned.' Is that

an idiom saying?" a third student said. That led us into a lengthy discussion about how not spending a penny you already have is the same as earning another penny you do not yet have.

"I haven't seen all of you think this much since Moby Dick was a guppy," I said at the end of the class period.

"Huh?"

"That's an idiom too; it means ..."

"Who's that Moby guy?" someone interrupted just as the dismissal bell rang. Thank you, Jesus.

The next morning, by the time my first-period class of sixth graders arrived, I had written on the board: *You are barking up the wrong tree.*

First words out of the mouth of the first kid to enter the classroom: "What's that?"

"That's your daily one-question quiz."

"What's it mean?"

"That's my question to you. That's what makes it a *quiz.*"

We spent the better part of each class period that day discussing that idiom, and others. We even started a list. The boys' favorite idioms were "Beat you to the punch," and "The ball is in your court." Duh! The girls' *least* favorites were "Don't let the cat out of the bag," "Curiosity killed the cat," and "More than one way to skin a cat." Lavenia wanted to know why they were picking on cats so much. They all, boys and girls alike, thought, "You can't cut the mustard," was an idiotic idiom. But the one that created the most, and the most interesting, discussion was "Elvis has left the building." I was surprised by how popular Elvis was with their generation, thirty years after he died.

One particular day, when Arianna entered the classroom, she marched straight to the board and wrote, "He is so ghetto," beneath where I had already written "Caught between two stools," as that day's one-question quiz.

"What's that?" someone asked her, as soon as everyone settled down.

"It's an idiom," Adrianna indignantly replied, then looked over at me. "It means..."

"I know what it means," I said, interrupting her. "And it is really more of a derogatory slang expression than an idiomatic phrase."

"I just like saying that word: Id..i...om," Lavenia said.

Saved by the Belle.

35

FROM THE MOUTHS OF BABES

Above The Fray

ONE OF THE MOST IMPORTANT THINGS ALL TEACHERS HAD TO do on the first day of each new school year was assign locker numbers.

"I want each of you, starting with the orange table, then the yellow table, and so on around the room, to come up here to my desk so I can give each of you the number and combination of your assigned locker," I said. "I also have a few words of warning: First, do not share your combination with anyone, unless you also want to share your belongings with them; and second, do not replace the school's combination lock with one of your own. If you do, Mr. Callaghan will cut them off with his big bolt cutters, in a heartbeat."

On the fourth day of school, before getting class underway, I asked if anyone had experienced any problems opening his or her locker. At first, no one reacted or responded. Finally, Juan, the smallest sixth grader I ever taught, slowly eased his hand above his head, but didn't speak.

"Juan, is your combination not working; can you not open your locker?" I coaxed.

"I don't know," he timidly replied.

"How can you not know? It's our fourth day of school?"

"I can't reach it," he calmly admitted.

"I'll trade lockers with Juan," Gabriella offered, before I figured out what to say. "Mine is a bottom locker; his is on top," she said.

You Don't Say

CLASS WAS ABOUT TO END. THE KIDS WERE PACKING UP, preparing to move on to fifth period. I was roaming the classroom, checking for pencils-on-the-floor hazards.

"Mr. Massey, you know what sucks?" Courtney matter-of-factly asked as I passed her seat at the yellow table.

"I don't know, Courtney; what sucks?" I replied, expecting a punch line.

"Breaking up with the boy you've been dating since second grade," she solemnly said while stuffing her purse into her backpack.

"Who is this crazy person, that let you get away? Do I know him?" I asked, with a bit more sympathy.

"I'm not tellin'."

I wanted to say something consolingly appropriate but

was distracted by thoughts of when I was in second grade, and had a crush on Ann Smith, who never knew I existed.

The dismissal bell rang, I dismissed them, and the kids started filing out of the classroom. "Courtney?" I called out and motioned her over as she walked past my desk.

"Sir?"

"You've got me curious; where did you go on dates in second grade?"

"Oh, we didn't ever go anywhere. That's just what we say when we like somebody, a lot."

Hmm. Ann Smith grew into a smart and beautiful woman; wonder if I can claim we dated in second grade?

A Fish Tale

FOR ABOUT FIVE YEARS DURING THE MID-STAGE OF MY teaching career, we kept a succession of betta fish in our classroom. They served as mini-mascots for us and resided in a large bowl on the front edge of my desk. My original intent was to add an element of low-maintenance pet life to my corner desk area. I had tried houseplants there, but even philodendrons could not survive the meager sunlight, and those things would usually flourish in a closet.

Hoping to instill a fun-related daily responsibility into my students' days, each was allowed, or required, as the case may be, to feed the fish in accordance with a posted schedule. The schedule was arranged in such a way that the student who had fed the fish the previous day, could remind the student seated across from, beside, or behind him or her that "Today is your day to feed Betahoven."

I wish I could lay claim to so cleverly naming our mascot, but some of the kids

extemporaneously came up with it. The name Betahoven surfaced one day, and stuck.

On the last day of each school year, all students who chose to do so, could put his or her—usually the hers—name in a hat from which we drew the name of the lucky new adoptive owner of Betahoven. Such was the fate of Betahoven I and II, but Betahoven III was less fortunate. In first period, one day near the beginning of fourth quarter, Anton asked if he could use my stapler. The kids knew, under threat of being exiled to a math class, they were not to use or remove anything from my desk without my expressed permission. "I won't take anything out of your backpacks, if you don't take anything off my desk," is the agreement I make with them on day one.

When Anton got to my desk he suddenly announced loud enough for all to hear, "Hey! Mr. Massey. Betahoven looks *decreased.*" When I looked over, he was poking at the fish with his fingertip. The fish was bobbing like a cork. I had not noticed, earlier.

While the kids worked on the daily one-question quiz, I slipped out of the room to unceremoniously dispense with Betahoven III. When I returned to the classroom, I had a quiet discussion with Anton. I explained the difference between decreased and deceased. He pointed out the vague similarities.

Once we had completed the daily one-question quiz, class captain Joy collected everyone's papers, brought them to me, and returned to her seat beside Allyson at the orange table; the table nearest my desk.

"We had a betta fish once. I named him Toto because I wanted a puppy but wasn't allowed to have a dog. But Toto committed suicide," I overheard Allyson inform Joy.

"Huh? He did what?" Joy inquired. At that point, I went from merely overhearing their conversation, to outright eavesdropping on them.

"He committed suicide," Allyson calmly and casually repeated.

"How? When?" Joy wanted to know. So did I.

"We went to Walmart one Saturday afternoon, and when we got back home, Toto had jumped out of his bowl and was lying on the table, stiff-as-a-board dead. My momma flushed him down the toilet."

"That doesn't mean he committed *suicide*," Joy asserted.

"Well, he knew he couldn't live outside that bowl, but he jumped out anyway," Allyson reasoned.

Timing Is Everything

I HAD OCCASION TO TEACH SEVERAL SETS OF IDENTICAL TWINS over the years, but none more identical than Tamara and Tamera. I taught them for two years, as both seventh and eighth graders, but fortunately never together in the same class period. I am certain those young ladies could have, and probably did, engage in acts of deception under the guise of being the other one. I wondered what life was going to be like for Tamara's and Tamera's eventual boyfriends. I foresaw deviousness in their futures.

"I saw you at the mall with Jake last Saturday afternoon!"

"Wasn't me. It was Tamera."

"You *are* Tamera!"

"Are you sure about that?"

One day toward the end of their seventh-grade year, I took a group of kids on a field trip to the North Carolina Museum of Art. On our way back to school, Tamara was sitting across the aisle from me near the front of the bus. Tamera was sitting somewhere behind us. We could hear her laughing.

"So, Tamara, what's it like having a twin?" I asked, genuinely interested.

"Pretty cool and pretty weird."

"Cool, how?"

"Whenever she gets something new, like clothes, it's like I get them too, because we share."

"And weird, how?"

"She seems to always have on the outfit I want to wear."

"Does your mom or dad have trouble telling you apart?"

"Oh no; I wish they did. If one of us so much as sneezes from the other end of our house, they can tell which one of us did it."

"Which of you was born first; who is oldest?"

"She is. By five minutes."

"So tell me, Tamara, how did you get to be so much smarter, and more talented, and prettier than your sister?" I joked.

Tamara didn't speak for about twenty solemn seconds. She

didn't even change her expression. Then she looked me straight in the eye, and said, "Them extra five minutes must have been really important, huh?"

Oh, Don't Be So Silly

OUR SCHOOL HAD FOUR CUSTODIANS, ONE FOR EACH WING OF our building. All were also school bus drivers, and all but one, Mrs. Comer, were men.

One thing I always loved about being a teacher was the mutual respect we had for one another; how everyone called everyone else Mr., Mrs., Ms., or Miss. No one called me Bill, and I didn't call anyone by his or her first name. And the custodians were not exceptions.

Mrs. Comer, a single parent, had two sons. Her oldest was in high school. Her

youngest, TJ, was in my second-period sixth-grade class. He was a gregarious and fun-loving kid, who immensely respected his "Momma." When she left school at the end of the day to run her school bus route, which took about an hour, TJ stayed behind at school and emptied all the waste-baskets in every classroom in her assigned wing of the school.

One day in class, I noticed TJ was showing another student an aerosol can of that

Silly String stuff kids loved to squirt all over everything, especially each other. When he looked across the room at me, I gave him a look, and made a "Put that away, now," gesture. He hurriedly stuffed it into his backpack.

Later that day, after school, while his momma was still out on her bus route, I

encountered TJ in the hallway outside a C-Hall classroom. He was dumping a wastebasket into a big on-rollers trashcan. Uncharacteristically, he did not speak as I approached.

"How're you doing TJ?" I asked, as I walked past.

"Not so good, Mr. Massey," he replied, I could tell he meant it. So, I stopped and

turned back.

"What's wrong, TJ?"

"You know that can of Silly String you saw me with in your class today?" he

asked. I nodded. "Well, I bought it at the mall last night, and this morning my momma said, 'TJ, if you know what's good for you, you won't be taking that mess to school today.'"

"But you did, anyway," I guessed.

"Yes, Sir. And in fourth period, one of my friends took it out of my backpack and

sprayed it in Mrs. Roberts' classroom," TJ said, shaking his head in regret.

"And?"

"And Mrs. Roberts got mad and took me to Mr. Callaghan's office, and Mr.

Callaghan got mad and called my momma to his office, and she got mad and asked Mr. Callaghan if she could use his office, and ... and ... " TJ stopped in mid-sentence and shook his head some more.

"And ... what?" I asked, after waiting a long moment.

"And she took a belt ... and ... and ... I thought my momma

was never gonna stop whuppin' me, Mr. Massey," he confessed, and teared up.

"What about your friend, the one who sprayed the Silly String? What happened to him?" I asked, trying to sound sympathetic.

"He ain't my friend no more."

Years later, on a Sunday morning, as I sat in my favorite chair drinking coffee and watching Charles Osgood on *CBS Sunday Morning*, my cell phone rang. It was an unfamiliar number, but I answered anyway; something I didn't usually do.

"Mr. Massey?" the caller asked.

"Who's calling?"

"It's me, TJ. Remember me?" I had not heard from TJ since he left middle school for high school.

"Of course, I do. And I remember the Silly String episode," I teased.

"Me too. Believe me," TJ said, and laughed out loud.

"Where are you? You sound close by."

"Well I ain't. I'm in Kuwait. I'm in the army."

"What are you doing in Kuwait?"

"We're staging to maybe go back into Iraq; we don't really know," he replied, as if resigned to that eventuality.

"But we're not supposed to be putting more boots on the ground in Iraq; that's what President Obama said," I pointed out.

"Maybe he's gonna let us wear our sneakers," TJ replied, and laughed again.

Vintage TJ.

A couple of years after that, I met TJ for dinner at a restaurant in Raleigh. He had

recently been honorably discharged from the army. A year later, TJ called me again—to proudly tell me he had a wife, and a son.

"How does your momma feel about being a grandma?"

"I think she wants to take a belt to me, again," he replied. I knew he was smiling ear to ear; I could picture it.

Friends To The End

"WALK WITH ME DOWN TO MY CLASSROOM FOR A MINUTE. I want to show you something," my friend and partner-in-academic-torment said as we reentered the building after an always-dreaded stint on after-school carpool duty.

When we entered his classroom, Boyce removed a stack of end-of-chapter Earth

Science test papers from his desk drawer, rolled off a rubber band, and started shuffling through them. As he did, I noticed the test was on the subject of tectonic plates.

"You're going to love this," Boyce said, with a chuckle. He knew I had a vested interest in the outcomes of his tests because I helped him remediate some of his students for retesting, following poor test performance the first time around.

He came across what he was looking for, pulled the two test papers from the stack, and handed them to me. I immediately noticed the two young ladies—both of whom were also in my class—had monumentally failed their tests with the exact same low-fifties grade.

"They both missed the very same questions with the very same incorrect fill-in-the-blank answers, but swore they did not cheat, despite sitting side by side during the test," Boyce said.

I checked the first three incorrect answers, and indeed, they were identical ... including the same misspelling of two of their eleven wrong answers.

"Look at question number sixteen, on the second page. That's the doozy of all doozies," Boyce said.

The first test-taker's paper had listed as her answer to that question, "idk," which is an acronym for, "I don't know," in teen-talk. Apparently, three words is too much to write all the way out. The second test-taker's answer to that same question was, "Me neither."

The prosecution rests, Your Honor.

Another Brother; Another Mother

"HEY, BROTHER, WHAT'S UP?"

"Not much sis, what's up with you?"

For some reason, near the beginning of my second year of teaching, that is how my colleague, Mrs. Staton, who taught eighth-grade social studies, and I began addressing each other. No matter when or where—early morning bus duty, mid-day lunch monitoring, after school staff meetings, hallway encounters during class change—it was always, "Hey brother," and "Hi sis," regardless of who was present—kids, parents, our principal, or the superintendent. It became second nature with us.

Numerous times during each school year, she would be asked if I was really her brother, and I would be asked if she was really my sister. Our mutually agreed upon answer: "Yes, of course. We're twins, can't you tell?" That reply always evoked strange looks, but seldom resulted in follow-up questions. Primarily, I suppose, because she is five feet nothing and I am six feet five, and I am twenty-five years her senior.

Nonetheless, at one of our three annual parent/teacher conferences one school year, at the conclusion of her report card review with one of her students and his mother, the mother commented, "Now I have to go find Mr. Massey and discuss this grade in *his* class." Her tone, according to Mrs. Staton, was reflective of mild displeasure with her son, or me, or both of us.

"As soon as she said that, the boy leaned over and semi-whispered to his mother, 'Be careful what you say about Mr. Massey in front of Mrs. Staton, they're twins.' Between laughing and trying not to laugh, I almost fainted," Mrs. Staton reported to a group of us teachers congregated in the teacher workroom eating cold pizza after conferences had ended.

Oh, did I mention Mrs. Staton is black, and I am white?

36

DIAMONDS IN THE ROUGH

Polishing A Jewel

FOR SEVERAL YEARS, MY STEPDAUGHTER, ELIZABETH, WORKED for Lenovo, a large computer manufacturer located in Research Triangle Park, North Carolina. In keeping with their civic-mindedness, Lenovo affiliated itself with a community outreach program that refurbished desktop computers and donated them to children of low-income families. Elizabeth often volunteered there, helping prepare those computers for their eager new owners, and she put me in contact with Sylvia, the woman who coordinated that program.

"We would be glad to accommodate the needs of your students," Sylvia cheerfully told me in a telephone conversation.

"How many students?" I asked, implying we could use a bunch while trying not to sound greedy.

"How many of your students live in a home not equipped with a computer?"

The following day, without explaining why, I passed out photocopies of a simple quarter-page questionnaire to every student in all my classes. I had hand written the master copy, so they would appear less formal. The slips of paper read:

Please   print   your   name:

_____

Is there a properly functioning computer in your home? ____ *Yes* ____ *No*

Thank you.

"I'm not asking if you have your own computer in your room. I'm asking if *anyone* in your family has a computer anywhere in your home," I reiterated, as class captains passed out the slips.

"Why do you want to know?" someone asked in every class.

"For one thing, I want to know how many of you need time on the computers in our media center to do research for class assignments. So I can schedule it with Ms. Whitt."

"We're getting a new assignment?" was usually the veiled complaint, disguised as a follow-up question.

"Would you like one? I can hook you up," I would reply. No further comment.

As committed, I called Sylvia back after school with a headcount.

"I have twenty-two students without at-home access to a

computer," I reported, with slight trepidation. That seemed like a lot to ask. Sylvia did not seem to flinch at that number.

Having had a couple of days to line up my ducks, I asked Mr. Callaghan to summon those twenty-two kids to the school library during homeroom. I explained to the kids why we were there and handed out field trip permission slips.

"Do we have to go on a Saturday?" Jewel, one of my eighth graders, immediately asked, with a hint of an attitude.

"We don't *have* to go, at all," I said. Jewel frowned but said nothing else. The room hushed. I paused for a moment. "Yes. We must go on Saturday. It's the only day they do this," I announced to everyone. "We will go by school activity bus ... if ... you have returned your signed permission slip. If not ... bummer." I added, "We will leave here, from the bus lot, at 8:00 a.m., sharp. If you are not here by eight ... double bummer."

"Why so early?" Jewel moaned.

"Because I have to get back home in time to wash and dry my hair," I joked, trying to temper my displeasure.

When I dismissed everyone else to go back to homeroom, I asked Jewel to remain behind. "Jewel, have you ever heard the expression, 'Never look a gift horse in the mouth?'"

"No."

"What do you think it means?"

"I don't know," she snapped, as if she couldn't care less. I had planned to simply tell her what it meant, but quickly changed my mind.

"Come with me," I said, and led her into the media center, right next door.

"Ms. Whitt, may I please leave Jewel with you, until she looks something up on one of your computers, and writes it down?" Ms. Whitt handed Jewel a slip of paper and a pencil and directed her to the nearest computer. "Never look a gift horse in the mouth—what does it mean?" I repeated to Jewel. "Look it up. Write it down. Leave your answer with Ms. Whitt," I instructed.

I left the media center and went straight to the gym. "Miss Hilsey, Jewel will be a few minutes late for PE. She's in the media center getting an attitude adjustment," I explained, and apologized.

"Good luck with that," she replied.

Two Saturday mornings later, we departed school at eight o'clock, sharp. All twenty-two students were onboard. When we arrived at the computer distribution site, the kids were warmly greeted with milk or juice and cookies and welcomed by Sylvia. "When you finish your snacks, we have a short information sheet we would appreciate you filling out, so we can get to know you better," she said.

Pens and forms on clipboards were passed out and the kids set about filling them out while me, Gerry, and coach Kozak, our school's athletic director and our bus driver that day—the kids called her Coach K—floated about answering questions and helping decipher "big words."

At one point, Edwardo, a smallish sixth grader, sidled over to me looking pensive, almost in tears. He motioned for me to bend down.

"Mr. Massey, this says for me to sign my name. I don't know how to sign my name ... not in cursive. But I can print it," he whispered.

"Just print it; that'll be okay," I assured him.

You could have measured the smile that spread across his face with a Geiger counter. "I was scared they weren't going to let me have a computer," Edwardo admitted.

Note:
The following week, we spent a full period in each class, the kids excitedly learning to sign their names in cursive. "I don't want you to ever turn in another quiz or assignment with your name printed. Sign your name; you now know how," I told them. Their pride was palpable. To paraphrase Winston Churchill, that class period may have been their "finest hour."

As soon as forms were completed and submitted, the kids were taken five at a time into a large classroom. Each was assigned a service technician who spent twenty to thirty minutes with them, teaching them how to correctly configure their computers—which cable connected where—and how to fire-up the system and perform basic operational functions—creating a new Word document, opening an internet browser, accessing PowerPoint and Excel, saving their work, and properly shutting down their computer.

"Okay, it's all yours," the techs told beaming-faced kids, before helping them disconnect, bubble wrap, package, and label their box with their name, before helping load their newly acquired computer system—monitor, CPU, keyboard, mouse—into the back of our bus.

All went well during that process, until Jewel was called in for her instruction session and pitched a fit when she discovered she wasn't getting a laptop.

"Laptops are not part of our program," I heard the tech politely explain.

"I don't want a (expletive deleted) desktop computer," Jewel loudly proclaimed, before jumping up, storming back out to the lobby, slamming herself down into a chair, and folding her arms in pouted-lip defiance. There was stone cold silence for a long moment. The kids were all staring at me.

"Jewel, come with me. You and I are going to go sit on the bus until everyone else has gotten his or her computer. As for you, you're getting your vulgarly-laced wish—you're *not* getting one," I said, barely concealing my anger.

"I'll take her to the bus and sit with her. You stay here with the other kids," Coach K offered.

That was not my first encounter with Jewel's defiance. Two summers earlier, Mr. Callaghan had asked if I would consider teaching an AVID class to a select group of seventh graders the upcoming school year. AVID (Advancement Via Individual Determination) is a widely known, proven to be effective program aimed at helping kids prepare for college, starting as early as middle school.

"But you'll have to give up your planning period to do it," he warned. "That's the only time available, and central office will never authorize giving up one of your art classes."

"That's how I spend my planning periods now ... trying to figure out how to get through to these knot-heads," I half-joked.

"I have a federal grant to pay for it, at least for the first year, including the expense of your training in Sacramento, the first week of July," Mr. Callaghan casually slipped into our conversation.

The third week of July, Mr. Callaghan and I, with input from other teachers, selected thirty-two rising seventh-grade students to be enrolled in my AVID class. Jewel was one of them.

"That's a lot of kids to have in one class," Mr. Callaghan said.

"Not if they know to behave themselves," I said.

It was only the second week of school when I put Jewel out of AVID class for repeatedly being disruptive and replaced her with one of the kids on our waiting list. And it was only a matter of days after that before Jewel, being unhappy with the keyboarding class into which she had been transferred, came knocking on my classroom door.

"If you will let me back into AVID, I promise I will behave, everyday," she said.

"Why do you want back in?" I asked. No immediate answer. "Where are you supposed to be, right now?"

"Mrs. Toler's class."

"Does Mrs. Toler know where you are?" No reply. "Is that what you call 'behaving'—skipping her class to come talk to me about the new leaf you've turned?" No reply. "I'm sorry Jewel, but, as my grandma used to say to me, 'I don't accept promises for future behavior.'"

Our AVID money ran out at the end of that first year and the grant was not renewed, so the program was discontinued at our school. A shame.

When I went to the bus after thanking Sylvia and her staff for the generosity of their time and gracious patience with the kids, everyone was loaded onboard, waiting, ready to head back to school.

"Jewel, come with me," I said, as soon as I counted heads.

"Where to?"

"You and I are going back in there, and you're going to apologize to that young woman who was trying to help you. The woman you cursed." Jewel didn't budge. "If not, I'm going to call your mother, and we are all going to wait right here on this bus until she comes to pick you up to take you home, after *she* takes you in there to apologize." Jewel sat, arms folded, glaring at me like a demon.

"Coach, I'm going back inside to call her mother. I'll be right back," I explained. Coach K pulled the handle that opened the bus doors. I stepped off. Jewel followed.

The technician was quite gracious in accepting Jewel's begrudging apology.

On our way back to school, as previously promised, we stopped at a McDonald's for lunch.

"Coach K, Gerry, please take the kids inside. And will one of you please bring Jewel something for lunch, when you return?" I asked and held out a ten-dollar bill.

Coach K took it, and asked, "Jewel, what would you like?" Jewel refused to answer. "What would *you* like, Mr. Massey," she asked, turning to me.

"A Quarter Pounder, with cheese, and a Diet Coke, please."

"Fries?"

"Oh ... why not?"

In about ten minutes, Coach K reentered the bus. She handed me a Mickey-D's bag containing my order. She also handed Jewel a bag. I have no idea what was in it, but Jewel ate it.

When we got back to school, most parents were waiting.

"You sit right here, until I help the other students load their computers into their parents' cars," I instructed Jewel. That task took about ten minutes. Once it was done, I fetched Jewel from the bus and walked with her over to where her mother was waiting in her car.

"Jewel is not getting a computer," I said, bluntly.

"What? Why not?" her mother asked, turning to glare at her daughter.

"Why not, Jewel? Your mother asked you a question?" She didn't speak. So I did. "Jewel was unhappy with the *free* computer she was being offered, so she cursed at the person trying to assist her, then threw a tantrum that embarrassed her classmates, the chaperones, and me, and shamed our school. I doubt we will ever be invited back."

"Jewel, go get in my car and pray to God I don't get there any time soon," her mother snapped.

Two weeks later, I called Jewel's mother at her work. "I have Jewel's computer here in our supply room. It was on the bus with us that Saturday, but Jewel didn't know it," I explained. "Will you be able to stop by school and pick it up, sometime soon?"

"Does she know you have it?" her mother asked.

"No. I'm going to let you tell her, and give it to her, whenever and however you see fit."

Jewel never mentioned her computer to me, nor I to her. At the end of the school year she moved on to high school and we lost touch until the end of her senior year, when she called me at school.

"Mr. Massey, it's Jewel; remember me?" *Oh, yeah!* I thought.

"Of course I do. How are you?"

"If I send you one of my invitations (she was only allotted four) will you come to my graduation?" she cheerfully asked. Gerry and I went to the ceremony a few weeks later. Afterwards, I gave Jewel a hug and wished her well. I have not heard from her since.

Destiney's Destiny

ONE SUNDAY EVENING, DURING MY FOURTH YEAR OF TEACHING, Gerry and I watched a *60 Minutes* segment about the burgeoning numbers of homeless students attending Florida public schools—specifically in Orlando. It was heartbreaking. Especially the story about Destiny, a sixth grader who lived with her mom, dad, and two brothers—one older, one younger—in their family's van.

The next day at school, I pulled the segment up on YouTube and we watched it in all six of my classes.

The video revealed that after sleeping in the van in an Orlando area shopping center parking lot each night, Destiny would go into the restroom of a Walmart every morning to brush her teeth and wash up before heading to classes at her middle school where, despite all odds, she was an honor roll student.

"What is it like for you, living in your van?" the interviewer asked Destiny.

"It's better than not having a van to live in," she politely replied. She even managed a smile.

Because of the age similarity, her story resonated more

personally with my sixth graders than the seventh or eighth graders, and with the girls more than the boys. When the video ended, there were a lot of damp eyes. Mine included. Again.

"Someone needs to help her," Kirsten said, solemnly, after a long moment of sniffle-punctuated silence.

"No! No! She is *our* age. *We* need to help her," someone else immediately exclaimed. Oddly enough, or perhaps not, it was Destiney, spelled "with an e," as she was always quick to point out.

Destiney was a small, quiet student who usually had very little to say. But when she did speak up, she was most often profound. Specifically, I recall the time we were discussing a Norman Rockwell painting in which a small boy discovers a Santa Claus suit in his dad's bureau drawer.

"How can kids believe Santa can go all around the world in one night?" someone smirked.

"Because they know he is magical!" Destiney immediately snapped back with obvious disdain for the sarcastic doubter. Dynamite in a small package.

On another occasion, I was explaining to the kids that when my mother died, even though it was late August, she left behind my Christmas present, a small package, wrapped and tagged—To: Billy, Love: Mother—and hidden away in her closet till Christmas. I found it when we cleaned out her house a few weeks after her funeral.

"Here it is ... unopened ... after almost thirty years," I said, holding up the frayed and faded package. "I have no idea what's in this box; no one does," I explained, before letting the kids pass it around. Almost all of them shook it and listened for a rattle. Many ventured guesses as to its contents.

"It's too big to be socks ... unless it's a bunch of 'em."

"Maybe it's a tie."

"If it's candy, like chocolate covered cherries, or them chocolate bells with crème inside, it's gross by now. Yuck!"

Someone suggested it was probably a gift card that had expired. "Wrapped in a big box, to fool you." I reminded them that gift cards were not "a thing" back then.

"Where do you keep it?" Destiney asked.

"In my closet. I put it under our tree every Christmas, then put it back on the closet shelf after we've opened all the other gifts."

"Why don't you open this one?" several students wanted to know.

"Because by keeping my mom's gift a secret, it helps keep my memory of her alive, in some odd way."

"What will happen to it when you die?" Destiney asked, in a tone that reflected more concern than curiosity.

"Hmm ... Good question. I hadn't thought about that, but I sup..."

"You should have it put in your coffin, and have it buried with you," Destiney interrupted me to suggest. That is now my plan.

"How would you like to help her ... help Destiny?" I asked. No one spoke up. "Kirsten you suggested it first; any ideas?"

"I don't know what she needs. She is way down there in Florida, and we are way up here," Kristie admitted.

"Destiney, what do you think?"

"We should invite her to come visit us ... and ask her how

we can help," Destiney emphatically proposed. Everyone looked at me for a reaction. "I wonder if she spells her name with an *e* ... like me?" Destiney said, as if thinking out loud.

"If we invite her to visit, and she wants to come, and her parents agree, we have to be prepared to pay her way," I reminded them.

During my lunch period that afternoon, I called the principal at Destiny's school in Orlando and explained that my students in North Carolina had seen the story of Destiny's plight on *60 Minutes* and wanted to write to her, to express their admiration and offer encouragement. The principal put me in touch with his school's guidance counselor, Ms. DeMarco.

"That would be lovely. Destiny will be thrilled. If you mail their letters to my attention, I will see to it that Destiny gets them, straight away," Ms. DeMarco promised.

The following day I informed my sixth-grade girls' L2L class—Kristie's and Destiney's group—of my conversations with Destiny's principal and guidance counselor. "Her name is Ms. DeMarco," I said.

"Is she as nice as our counselor, Ms. Currin?" someone wanted to know.

"*Now* can we ask Destiny to come visit us?" Destiney persisted.

"This afternoon, I will call to find out roughly how much round-trip airfare from Orlando to Raleigh would be. The last thing we want to do is invite her to visit, then renege because it's too expensive," I said, then asked, "Who knows what renege means?"

"To be an Indian giver," someone shouted out.

"In the meantime, I want you ladies … *all* of you, not just one or two of you … to brainstorm and make a list on the board of all the things we need to consider in order to pull this off. You have till the end of this class period."

"I'm going to do the writing,'" Kristie said, and rushed to the board.

"Oh ... and by the way, Destiney with an *e* ... Ms. DeMarco said Destiny spells her name without an *e*," I said. Destiney seemed a bit disappointed.

When the class dismissal bell rang, the following list was scribbled on the board:

- Get her parents' permission.
- Find out when she can come.
- How long can she stay?
- Where will she stay?
- What will she do while we are in our classes on school days?
- What will we do to entertain her while she is here?
- How much food money will she need?
- How much spending money?
- How much will airplane ticket cost?
- How can we help her when she goes home, without embarrassing her?

For lunch that day, I joined some of my colleagues at the teachers' table in the school cafeteria where I was introduced to a substitute teacher who was filling in for Ms. Dawes. I was telling them about the *60 Minutes* report on the effects of homelessness upon so many school children in Florida, and about Destiny.

"I saw that *60 Minutes* segment. It was heartbreaking," one of my fellow teachers

said.

"Well my kids are damned and determined to do something to help Destiny," I

said. "They want her to come visit them."

"Calling your students *kids* makes them sound like baby goats," the sub

chimed in. Her only utterance since I sat down to join them.

"And calling them *students* makes them sound like total strangers," I countered,

perhaps more acerbically than was called for. But still.

As soon as school let out that afternoon, I went to the front office to use the

phone. Fifteen minutes later, when I walked back into my classroom I wrote

$293 beside the kids' question: "How much will airplane ticket cost?"

Within a matter of days, the kids had decided they could cover Destiny's food and fun money and pay part of her airfare by conducting a Krispy Kreme fundraising sale to parents, and by selling World's Best Chocolate candy bars to their schoolmates for $1 each. "Okay," Mr. Callaghan agreed. "But they cannot sell them before or during lunchtime," he warned.

"Don't worry about the airfare," I told the kids. "I will

work on covering that expense," I committed. The relief was visible on their faces.

"My mom said Destiny can stay at our house while she is here," Mary Anna offered.

Kristie sprang up, rushed to the board, and put big black check marks beside "How much is airfare?" and "Where will she stay?"

"I guess we'd better get started writing your letters to Destiny," I suggested. "Everyone take out a clean, unwrinkled sheet of notebook paper. Do not rip it out of your binders; no ragged holes, please."

I didn't care if the kids wrote in pen or in pencil. And while I loosely monitored the content of their letters, guiding them away from anything that might be naively hurtful, I tried not to stifle their youthful enthusiasm and optimism.

"Remember, we're writing to an honor roll student, so let's not be sloppy with our grammar and spelling," I pleaded.

In the end, I was pleased and proud of their sensitivity and compassion. I was particularly interested in seeing what Destiney might write. While most of the other girls were passionate about this undertaking, Destiney was obsessively so, in a good way; a dog with a bone.

We kind of have the same name, except mine has an e. But we definitely don't

have the same life. Yours is much harder than mine, and you still make honor roll.

I am so proud of you.

That is how Destiney opened her letter.

I took all twenty-seven letters home with me on Friday and read them one last time over the weekend, just to be sure.

On Monday, by the time the girls came into L2L class, I had written the name of Destiny's school on the board, along with the mailing address.

For the first half of the class period, anyone who wanted to do so read their own letter to the class. Most of them did. When they finished, Destiney and Kristie addressed a big envelope to Ms. DeMarco's attention and inserted the stack of their letters, along with one I had written, to the counselor.

Please feel free to read these, to ensure no offense is done to sensitivities of which my students are unaware.

On the outside back of the envelope, in red marker, Destiney wrote, *You are our hero!* Kristie sealed and taped the envelope securely shut, and the two of them marched it to the office and asked Mrs. Fields to add postage and mailed it.

"Mrs. Field's said tell you you owe her a Snickers, and not one of the little ones," Kristie said when they returned to class.

About the middle of the following week, Ms. DeMarco called and left a message for me with Mrs. Love. I returned her call after school.

"The letters arrived yesterday. They were both heart-warming and heartbreaking. I gave them to Destiny just before school dismissed. She was totally surprised, and said she wanted to read them alone. I saw her today but didn't get to speak with her.

"Would you mind contacting her parents, giving them my number here at school, and asking them to call me, please?"

The next morning, I told the kids Destiny had received their letters.

"What did she say?"

"She just received them, day before yesterday. It will take her a while to read twenty-seven letters. But Ms. DeMarco said she was very happy to get them."

"Have we heard from Destiny yet?" "Have we heard from Destiny yet?" I was asked that question several times a day, everyday for two weeks. Finally, a letter addressed to, "Mr. Massey's Students," written in a neatly deliberate cursive handwriting arrived from Orlando. The kids passed the unopened envelope around the room, each one handling it carefully, until it made its way back to me.

"Destiney, would you like to read Destiny's letter to the class?"

"No. You do it. You'll do it better."

"I'll do it," Kristie offered.

Destiny started her six-page letter, *Dear new best friends in North Carolina.* She then went on to mention each girl in our class by name, and comment on something that particular student had said in her individual letter. Several girls got up to fetch a handful of Kleenex from the box on my desk while Kristie was reading Destiny's letter. She closed her letter with, *Adults are usually the ones who are kind and sympathetic; kids can be so mean. But all of you seem different, and special. You certainly are to me.*

"*Now* can we invite Destiny to visit us ... please?" someone asked, with a tone of insistence. I had not allowed them to invite her in their letters. "We don't want to get her hopes up, only to have her parents say 'No,' and disappoint her," I had told them beforehand.

The next day, Mrs. Love paged me in my classroom during one of my seventh-grade classes. "Mr. Massey, I have a call on hold for you, from Orlando. Mrs. Currin is on her way down to your classroom to monitor your students while you come take it."

The call was from Destiny's father, David. He thanked me and asked me to "Thank those girls for making Destiny feel so special." I asked if we could invite her to come visit us, suggesting her spring break might be a good time—I already knew her break did not coincide with ours—so she could come spend time in our school. Mr. Callaghan had already agreed she could attend with my students for a week. I made sure to make mention to David that we would cover the expense of her trip. I didn't want to put him in the embarrassing position of having to say they could not afford it. He said Destiny would be thrilled by the invitation, that he would discuss it with her mom, and then get back to me. I gave him my cell number. He called me that evening.

"We ... her mom, her brothers, and I ... would like to drive Destiny to North Carolina. We would feel more comfortable that way; seeing where she would be, and who she would be with," David offered. I assured him that was perfectly understandable, and preferable. "We would only stay a day or two, then drive back to Florida, leaving her there to fly home later," David said. I told him we would provide gas money and agreed to arrange hotel accommodations for all of them.

"Destiny will be coming to visit us during her spring break; that's the week before your spring break," I told the girls the day after David and I had worked out the details. Everyone cheered and applauded. I had never seen a group of kids—or adults, for that matter—so determined to make something happen.

Destiny and her family arrived in Raleigh on a Sunday afternoon. I met them at the hotel where they would be staying, courtesy of my friend Eric and his company, Summit Hospitality Group. They had donated two rooms for two nights.

On Monday morning, Destiny and her family followed me to school. Destiney and Kristie met them in the lobby and presented Destiny with a new L2L t-shirt. She immediately put it on. While I went to prepare for homeroom, Mr. Callaghan gave Destiny and her family a tour of our school. When first-period bell rang, Destiney and Kristie brought them all to our L2L class. Kristie escorted Destiny's mom, dad, and brothers to a table in the back of the classroom, while Destiney stood with Destiny at the classroom door where hugs and giddy giggles were exchanged with each girl as she arrived at class. When the tardy bell rang, Destiney took a seat at the end of the yellow table, with Destiney and Kristie, and proceeded to take that day's one-question quiz, like all the other girls. (Every day that week, Destiny sat at a different table with a different group of girls; her idea.)

At lunchtime, one of our guidance counselors and two of the students' mothers took the family out to lunch, then on a tour of our small but historic town. Destiny ate in the cafeteria with the class, then spent the entire afternoon going with the girls from class to class. After school, Destiny bade her family goodbye; they were returning to Orlando bright and early the next morning. Hugs and handshakes were exchanged, gratitude was expressed, and Destiny's parents headed back to the hotel in Raleigh. Destiny went home with

Mary Anna. "She'll be fine," Mary Anna's mom assured her mom and dad.

Really early the following morning, I stopped by the hotel to ensure there would be no snags with the bill when Destiny's family checked out. "It's all squared away," the front desk clerk assured me.

Destiny spent the rest of the week being an "honorary student" of our school. Every teacher welcomed her into their classes and treated her like one of the gang.

Friday afternoon my Gerry and I treated the entire sixth-grade girls' L2L class to a cookout at our home in Raleigh.

"Mr. Massey, we thought you would have a bigger house. It's really nice, but it ain't big," the first group of girls agreed when they arrived with one of the parents.

"It's big enough. If you don't believe me, one of you can vacuum it."

Before hamburgers and chicken thighs were grilled and hot dogs and marshmallows were roasted, the girls took two perfectly good fresh loaves of bread to the lake in the city park behind our house and fed the massive gaggle of "ducks."

"They're not ducks; those are *geese*; from Canada," someone correctly pointed out.

"Can we walk around the lake?" they enthusiastically asked; enthusiasm that progressively waned as they got farther and farther into the two-mile circular trek.

On Saturday, Gerry and I took Destiny, Mary Anna, and her younger sister Sara, and Kristie (Destiney's mom would not let her go) to Pilot Mountain. and then to Mount Airy, the quaint North Carolina town that served as Mayberry for the filming of the popular *Andy Griffith Show* in the '60s.

Mid-afternoon on Sunday, Gerry and I took Destiny to RDU airport for her flight back to Orlando. When they called her flight, Destiny hugged and thanked us, then disappeared into the jetway. I spoke by phone with her dad a couple of times after their visit. As it turned out, Ellen DeGeneres had also been made aware of the *60 Minutes* story about Destiny and her family and she was helping them out.

We have not seen or heard from Destiny directly since her return to Florida. But I do know from her Facebook posts that she is currently a senior in high school and is still making honor roll grades.

Life Lesson Learned

ON THE MONDAY FOLLOWING DESTINY'S RETURN HOME TO Florida, the kids were somber. They obviously wanted to talk about her visit. I tried to stay out of the conversation and let the girls talk to each other.

"She didn't seem different from us."

"She didn't complain about her life, at all."

"She seemed happy. How could she be happy?"

"I'm never going to complain about my life again, that's for sure."

"What's gonna happen to her now?"

Those were a few of their comments, confessions, and concerns. But Destiney had not spoken, yet.

"There are probably kids like Destiny right here in our own school," she finally wondered, aloud. There were. Some known; some not.

"Mr. Massey, can we do a fundraiser, to help buy food for our school's Food on Fridays backpack program?" the kids asked, as soon as they got to class on Tuesday.

Food on Fridays was a program created and conducted by our school's National Junior Honor Society students whereby kids in danger of having little, if anything, to eat at home on weekends were provided backpacks stocked with food to take home on Fridays. On Mondays, they returned the backpacks —donated by the local Walmart store—to be restocked and reissued the following weekend.

"What kind of fundraiser?"

"We want to sell raffle tickets ... for $1 apiece ... to win a $50 Walmart gift card in a drawing."

"Sell tickets where, and when?"

"In the hallway outside the cafeteria, during lunch period."

"Okay by me, but you will have to be the ones to ask Mr. Callaghan for his permission."

"We'll do it, me and Brittany," Kirsten offered. I gave them permission to go seek Mr. Callaghan's blessing. They were back in less than fifteen minutes.

"He said okay, but only during lunch period, and only two days a week," Kirsten said.

"And only for two weeks; he doesn't want more than one fundraiser going on at a time," Brittany added. "And he said he was proud of us."

Every Tuesday and Thursday for the next couple of weeks the kids set up a table at lunchtime and sold all 150 raffle tickets they had designed in class and produced on the copier.

"Who do we give the money to?" the kids eagerly asked after their last day selling raffle tickets. Prior to that, I had kept it locked in my desk drawer; a no-no according to Mrs. Fields. "All funds, of any kind, are to be turned in and receipted, daily," she scolded me.

"Whoever it is you give it to, what do you want that person to do with the money?"

"Uh ... buy food?" someone answered, sounding surprised by my question.

"Why don't I take a couple of you to Food Lion, and *you* buy the food, instead? That'll be more helpful than simply handing over the money."

The kids nominated Kirsten, Brittany, Ellen, and Destiney to do the grocery shopping. "Can all four of us go?" they asked, remembering I had said I would take a *couple* of them. They were getting better about listening.

That Friday afternoon I met with the girls at lunchtime. Kirsten, Brittany, and Ellen each gave me a signed permission letter from their parents.

"Where's Destiney?"

"Her mom won't let her go," Kirsten and Brittany said at the same time.

"Okay. In that case, I'll meet the three of you here, on Monday, at 3:30, and we'll head out," I said. "And by the way, this is my contribution to your cause." I held out a $50 Walmart gift card the Walmart store manager had sold to me for $25. The girls looked perplexed. "Now you can spend all of your $150 on food," I explained.

On Monday, right after school, I took the three girls to a Food Lion store that was about two miles from our school.

"Don't forget to take a calculator with you, to keep tabs on how much you're spending as you go along," I instructed.

Brittany pulled one out of her purse and held it up. "Ta da!" she said, grinning.

Almost before the automatic doors had closed behind us at Food Lion, the kids had a grocery cart and were excited to get started.

"There is a whole aisle of discounted canned goods on that far wall," I pointed out. "You might want to start there, to maximize your buying power. And remember ... canned or packaged foods only. Don't get anything perishable."

"Are you going to help us?" Brittany asked.

"No. I'm not allowed to food shop. My wife says I buy too much junk food."

"Did you bring our money?" Ellen wanted to know.

"Right here," I said, and patted my shirt pocket.

"Can we buy some treats for them?" Kirsten wanted to know.

"Let's not start there," I suggested, and sent them on their way.

I stayed in the background, checking on them from afar, as they roamed up and down aisles. I also took advantage of the opportunity to replenish my stock of Bazooka bubble gum and bite-size Tootsie Rolls.

After almost forty-five minutes of giggly comparison-shopping, the girls checked in with me.

"We are up to $141. Can we buy them some cookies, now?"

"Fine. But buy small, individual size packs. You don't want a couple of kids getting five-pound boxes of Oreos, leaving nothing for anyone else."

"We ain't buying any Oreos," Brittany said, rather emphatically. "My momma won't buy 'em for me; says they're too expensive. And if I can't have 'em, I sure ain't buying 'em for someone else to eat."

"Hurry up. I'll wait for you up by the checkout lines, where there *ain't* nobody saying *ain't*," I said.

We loaded their purchases into the trunk of my car, and the girls piled in for the ride back to school. Before putting the key in the ignition, I pulled three six-cookie size packets of Oreos out of my jacket pocket and handed them to Brittany. She grinned, ear to ear. "You might want to share those with your friends, in the backseat," I said, and glanced in the rearview mirror at Kirsten and Ellen.

By the time we got back to school and transferred the grocery bags from my car into our classroom supply closet, the kids' parents were there to fetch them. The next morning, several of the kids each took a bag of groceries and proudly scurried off to the guidance counselor's office where the Food on Fridays pantry was located.

Three days later, during Friday morning announcements, the drawing was held, and Mr. Callaghan announced the raffle winner—one of the eighth-grade teachers—over the PA. About five minutes later, Mr. Callaghan was back on the PA, announcing that teacher was donating her $50 Walmart gift card to the Food on Fridays program.

Amanda's Gotta Do, What Amanda's Gotta Do

I MENTIONED EARLIER THAT MANY, IF NOT MOST, OF MY MIDDLE school students would in a skinny minute choose a root canal over reading a book. Not so with Amanda, whom I first met when she joined our before-school reading club as a sixth grader.

At the beginning of Amanda's seventh-grade school year, I noticed her in the school cafeteria one day. When I waved to her, she motioned me over to her table.

"I have a new book ... *Because of Winn-Dixie*," she beamed.

"Why would a grocery store be responsible for you having a new book?" I asked, half joking and half curious. I had not heard of the book.

"No. *Because of Winn-Dixie* is the name of my book. Here, see?"

She pulled the book out of her bag and held it out. I sat my tray down, took it, and started thumbing through the pages.

"It's about a ten-year-old girl named Opal who finds a stray dog she names Winn-Dixie, cause that's where she found him, in the parking lot at Winn-Dixie." I sat down across from her and ate my slice of too-salty pizza while she lamented how she was trying to learn to read better. "So I can go to college," she explained, without a hint of doubt that she could or would.

Before Amanda left the cafeteria, she and I had agreed I would get permission for her to bring her lunch into my classroom on Tuesdays and Thursdays, so she could read *Because of Winn-Dixie* to me. So I could help her with the "hard words," as she put it.

"Can I come on Wednesdays too?" she asked as she stood to leave the cafeteria. She was a gently persistent little soul.

"Sometimes, but not all the time. Some lunch periods I have to do paperwork."

Without fail, every Tuesday and Thursday Amanda was waiting at my classroom door, a smile on her face, a brown bag lunch and a book in hands, when I returned from the cafeteria with my lunch tray.

"We're starting on page thirty today," (... or forty-one ... or fifty-three ... or wherever we were to begin reading) was always the first thing she would say to me.

"Isn't that where we stopped last time? Aren't you reading at home, on your own?" I asked the first time she said that, as I fumbled with my keys to unlock the classroom door.

"I'm reading a Nancy Drew book at home right now. If I read this one on my own, you won't be able to follow the story."

About the third or fourth day we met, Amanda showed up without her brown bag.

"Where's your lunch? Aren't you eating today?" I asked, concerned.

"I ate last period, in my Study Island class. It's too hard to eat and read at the same time," she explained. "But I saved you a chocolate chip cookie. Made 'em myself, with lots of chocolate chips," Amanda said as she pulled a waxed-paper-wrapped cookie from her backpack and held it out.

"Wow! This is as big as a Frisbee, thanks," I remarked as I accepted it.

"It is not," she said, and grinned.

"Okay ... as big as a saucer," I relented.

One day in early spring, as she was leaving one of our lunchtime reading sessions, Amanda sheepishly handed me a small white sealed envelope. I flipped it over and noticed my name on the front in small, neat calligraphy.

"Did you write that?" I asked when I looked up, but Amanda was gone. I tore open the envelope and discovered a simple what-when-where invitation to her fourteenth birthday party. "Please try to come," was hand written at the bottom.

A few weeks later, on a sunny Saturday afternoon, Gerry and I left home in time to arrive at Amanda's house for her 2:00 p.m. party. I knew it was thirty-two miles from our house in Raleigh to our school in Oxford. What I did not know was that Amanda lived twelve miles beyond that, almost to the Virginia line. But no matter; she was thrilled to see us.

"I didn't think you would really come," she admitted.

"Of course I came—yours is the first official birthday party invitation I have gotten in an eon," I replied as I handed her a wrapped gift. "It's obviously a book; *The Tiger Rising*, by Kate DiCamillo, the author of *Because of Winn Dixie*," I said.

In the middle of her eighth-grade year, Amanda moved to Minnesota with her mom, dad, and younger brother and sister. Five years later, I received in the mail at school an invitation to Amanda's high school graduation. Unfortunately, a family medical emergency prevented me from attending; one of the deepest regrets of my teaching career. When I last heard from Amanda, she was in the process of enlisting in the US Army. "So I can qualify for college tuition benefits under the GI Bill," she explained. When I last tried to call Amanda, I was greeted by that dreaded robotic sounding "The number you have dialed has been changed or is no longer in service. Please check the number and try again," automated message.

Prima Donna

DONNA WAS ONE OF MY SIXTH-PERIOD ART CLASS STUDENTS; AN embittered eighth grader, and rightly so, perhaps. She was, as were many of my students, a ward of the Masonic Home for Children, formerly the Oxford Orphanage. The Masonic Home, though not ideal, was a Godsend for kids not in the custody of their parents for whatever reasons, including voluntary surrender. It was particularly heartbreaking when those kids spoke with hope and confidence of the day "My mom (or dad) comes back for me."

Donna went out of her way to be confrontational in all of her classes, with all of her teachers, but particularly with me, because I pushed back. She would intentionally show up for class late, and/or sit in another student's assigned seat, and/or be blatantly defiant and disruptive during class. Then she would pitch a profane hissy fit when I turned her away, required her to move to her own assigned seat, and/or expelled her from class and sent her to the principal's office.

"Mr. Massey, will you please come down to my office for a few minutes?" Mr. Allen, our assistant principal, requested over the intercom system. I was grading quiz papers and eating my lunch at my desk at the time.

When I got to his office, Donna was sitting in a chair outside his office door, her arms familiarly folded in walled-off defiance, her lips poked out in anger. I walked in and took a seat in one of the two chairs in front of Mr. Allen's desk. Without addressing me, he immediately called Donna in. She took the chair beside me, refolded her arms tightly across her chest, and stared past Mr. Allen, out the window behind him.

"So, Donna, what is your problem with Mr. Massey?" Mr. Allen calmly asked.

"He's an asshole," Donna said without hesitation, but with seeming certainty. Neither he nor I reacted. Both he and I had heard much worse from Donna.

"Perhaps you are seeing him that way because he's trying very hard to keep *you* from being that way," Mr. Allen suggested after a brief pause. "In which case, he would be a teacher asshole and you would be a student asshole, so he wound still be in charge," he added. Donna tried to ward off a smile, but it spread across her lips anyway. She tried to suppress a chuckle by cupping her hand over her mouth, but it slipped out between her fingers. Finally, she burst into loud, all-out snorting laughter. Then Mr. Allen started laughing, as only he could. Then I started laughing. After we regained our collective composure, Mr. Allen good-naturedly said, "You two assholes get out of here, and don't ever come back," causing Donna to have a guffaw relapse.

"What's so funny?" Ms. Currin asked when Donna and I came out of his office.

"Mr. Allen ... he's crazy," Donna exclaimed.

From that day forward, Donna never gave me a problem. She didn't become an honor roll student, but she stopped being an ... well ... you know what I mean.

On the last day of that school year, I summoned Donna to my classroom, and, knowing of her love for stringing beaded jewelry, gave her a jewelry-making kit the size of a fishing tackle box I had gotten at Michaels hobby and crafts store. She meekly thanked me, awkwardly hugged me, and moved on to high school.

Ashen Ashley

JUST AS HALF THE BOYS IN MY CLASSES HAD THEIR SIGHTS SET ON being an NBA or NFL star, half the girls were equally convinced they were destined to become a DVM—Doctor of Veterinary Medicine.

"Your first step toward becoming one is learning not to spell it v-e-t-t-e-r-n-a-r-i-a-n," I had to remind them as I wrote the correct spelling on the board. Then I would tell them, "I'm a vet," and they would shout, "No way!" and I'd say, "Yes, way. I'm a Vietnam vet," and they would hiss and boo. I was always more entertained by that little charade than they seemed to be.

No student in any of my classes was more determined to "Help sick or hurt animals," as she put it, than Ashley, a shy, bright seventh grader. She was always taking in strays or handing out treats. "I carry dog biscuits in my purse, just in case," she once told me. Then she pulled out a plastic sandwich bag filled with Friskies and showed me.

At the time, Gerry worked for the North Carolina Pork Council and knew a lot of pork producers—pig farmers— some of which became personal friends. (There are actually more pigs in North Carolina than people. Who knew?) One pair of such friends was H.D. and his wife Jan. H.D. served on the board of directors for the College of Veterinary Medicine at North Carolina State University. Jan was a former public-school teacher and current principal. Both were past presidents of the NC Pork Council.

With H.D.'s assistance and influence with Dean Warrick Arden's office, arrangements were made for me to take twenty of my students on a field trip to the vet school.

"With a group that small, your students will be able to go more places within the school and see more of what goes on behind the scenes," H.D. advised.

As soon as the trip was a definite "Go," I set about selecting twenty kids to be invited to make the thirty-two-mile trip to Raleigh.

"How many students are in your classes?" Gerry asked during a commercial break one night as we watched *NBC Nightly News*.

"In all six classes? One hundred sixty-nine."

"How are you going to fairly pick twenty?"

"They've already picked themselves. I'll show you, when the news is over."

As soon as Brian Williams invites us to join him for the news again the next night, I fetch my briefcase and remove a tall stack of papers; the personal-info questionnaires all my students filled out on the first day of school. I was interested in their answers to one of the twenty questions; the last question—"What do you want to be when you grow up?" Fifteen kids—twelve girls and three boys—had mentioned wanting to become vets.

"How will you select the other five?" Gerry asked.

"I'm going to invite the one student in each of my classes who has the highest grade-average in all of his or her core classes; if you don't have good grades, you're not getting into vet school."

On the morning of our field trip, I left most of my

students in the charge of a substitute teacher and headed out to the vet school with my other twenty-one kids. Some were wearing Wolfpack red t-shirts. None were wearing blue—neither light nor dark.

"Why didn't everybody have a chance to go?" That was the common reaction when I first explained to each class how I chose those who were invited.

"You *did* have a chance, all of you, when you filled out your personal questionnaires the first day of classes, back in August. This is an education-related activity, not a field trip to King's Dominion." That was my unpopular answer. "But, for the more artsy inclined among you, I'll try to arrange a visit to NC State's College of Art and Design, from which I graduated," I promised.

The dean's administrative assistant immediately greeted the kids upon our arrival at the vet school. She ushered us into a small auditorium, offered us juice or water, and informed us that, "Dean Arden will be in, momentarily."

The dean spent about thirty minutes with the kids. After welcomingly answering a few initial questions, he gave them the straight skinny on how they should start preparing themselves in sixth, seventh, and eighth grades. "If this is what you really want to do," he said.

"Excellent high school grades will get you past the first round of admissions consideration; get you into our *Possibly* stack of applications. But the foundation for good high school grades will, for the most part, be laid in middle school. So, the time to start applying yourself *is now*," he told them, then answered a few questions about the difference between good grades and *excellent grades*. The bottom line: Very few Bs. No Cs.

"How many of you are making excellent grades?" the dean inquired. The kids looked around at each other with dower faces, then looked at me, but none of them raised their hands. Not even the honor roll recipients or Junior Honor Society members.

"How many are capable of making excellent grades ... when you try?" I followed up. Smiles spread and hands shot up all over the room.

"We are the third ranked and one of only fourteen or so vet schools in the US. We get about 100 applications for each first-year enrollment slot. So, it's harder to get into vet school than into med school," he explained. "Now comes the important part," he continued. "To move your application from the *Possibly* stack to the *Probably* stack, we heavily consider past experiences working with and caring for animals."

"Like what?" someone asked.

"Like lots of things; growing up on a working farm, part-time job at an animal clinic, volunteer work at a rescue shelter, summer job as a pet-sitter or dog walker, nursing an ill or injured family pet."

"How many of you have done some of those things?" I asked the kids. Everyone smiled and raised their hands.

"But how will you know all that? Know what we did?" someone else asked the dean.

"You'll tell us. And here is the best and most impressive way to do that: Along with your application, submit a copy of a journal you have kept that talks about what you have done to improve the lives and health of animals—any animals—and when, and where, and how, and why," the dean said. "So, I suggest you start keeping such a journal now, if you don't already. That's how your application gets moved from the *Probable* stack to the *Definite* stack."

"Do any of you do that now; keep a journal?" I asked. Three or four students meekly raised their hands.

From the auditorium we were escorted to a laboratory where a professor and several students were intently focused on whatever it was they were doing, all huddled around one workstation. The professor left the group and greeted us, asking each of my students their first name, as he shook their hands. (Note to self: next time, nametags.)

After an informative tour of the lab, the professor led the kids to a metal, bookcase-like storage rack at the far end of the room. On the rack were glass jars filled with a slightly yellowish liquid, each containing an animal organ that was obviously a brain.

"What animal might this be the brain of?" he asked the kids as he held up the biggest one. "Correct," he exclaimed when someone finally guessed, "Horse." Then he held up other jars, in descending order of size, working his way down from cow, to sheep, to dog, to fox, to cat. Then he picked up the jar with the smallest brain.

"What do you think this is the brain of?" he asked. The kids made several guesses. "Nope." "Nope." "Nope," he said after each one, until all guesses were exhausted. "This ... is the brain ... of a Tarheel fan," he said with a dead-serious expression in a dead-serious tone. Some of the kids laughed, some booed. "Well ... I suppose it *could* be a squirrel," he said as he placed the jar back on the wire rack.

We left the lab and went straight to a fairly small room with a sign on the door that read: *Observatory*. On the other side of a large picture-window-size glass panel, a team of doctors and vet students were gathered around an operating table upon which lay a large German Shepherd that was obviously anesthetized. They were preparing to perform a knee replacement on the dog.

The kids all stared in silence, until the surgeon, who was visiting from France, was handed a scalpel which he used to carefully and slowly make the first incision on the animal's clean-shaven, left front leg. That's when some of the kids let out loud Ooos! ... Yucks!... and Grosses! And that's when Ashley fainted into the arms of several surprised classmates.

After sitting Ashley up and applying a cool, damp cloth to her forehead for a few minutes, until color began returning to her face, the very compassionate vet student who had been summoned to attend to her assisted me in getting a pale-as-Casper Ashley safely to a waiting area where she could lie down on a couch.

I stayed with Ashley while Mrs. Moore, a parent and chaperone, and Mr. Tunstall, our bus driver, escorted the kids on the remainder of their tour. After about fifteen minutes, ashen-colored Ashley sat up on the couch, turned and put her feet on the floor, and solemnly said, "Mr. Massey, I don't think I'd make a very good vet; do you?"

A few minutes later, Mrs. Moore was back. "The kids have been invited by some of the vet students to have lunch with them in the cafeteria. They're having pepperoni pizza." Ashley immediately made a gulping-gurgling sound as what little color she had regained again drained from her face. She turned, flopped back down on the couch, and put a hand over her eyes. "Oh brother," she mumbled.

"I'll stay with her," I said to Mrs. Moore.

A few days later, as the kids in each class worked on their one-question quizzes, I walked around the room giving each student who had gone on the vet school trip an inexpensive journal in which I had written: *Better get started, Good luck.* In third period, when I handed Ashley hers, she looked at me with a puzzled expression. I patted her on the shoulder and continued my rounds.

That was twelve years ago. Ashley could now be in her third year as a full-fledged Doctor of Veterinary Medicine by now. But in all likelihood, she is probably not a surgeon.

As promised, before the school year ended, with the support of Dean Marvin Malecha, arrangements were made for a group of my students—those that had listed "fashion designer" as a career choice on their personal info questionnaire at the beginning of the year, plus some who had exhibited notable artistic talent in class throughout the year—to tour NC State University's College of Art and Design.

At that time the college consisted of five different design programs—architecture, landscape architecture, industrial (product) design, graphic design, and art and design, the more fine-artsy of the five. So, on the day of our trip, when we arrived on campus at Brooks Hall, students from each design discipline greeted us to give the kids tours through their respective departments, all of which were abuzz with seemingly chaotic activity.

"Everyone is rushing to complete year-end final projects," our guide told us as we made our way past a dozen or so balsa wood and foam core models of buildings. "These guys are working on designs for an art museum," he added.

In the product design department, our tour guide introduced the kids to several students who explained they were working on designs for ski gloves with sensors in the fingertips that would allow for the use of cellphone touchscreens without removing the gloves. The kids were all over that idea, despite the fact that none of them had ever been close to a ski slope.

When we left the product design studio we were handed off to Gretchen, a fourth-year graphic design major with very pale skin and naturally bright-red buzz-cut hair. Some of the kids were enthralled by her small silver nose-ring, but all seemed enamored of her neck tattoo of a dragon whose head menacingly peered out from beneath the collar of her t-shirt. (It *was* kind of cool, though.)

"This place is a mess," one of the kids said to Gretchen as we strolled through a graphic design studio space. And it was. Every work surface and the floor, wall to wall, were strewn with balled up, wadded up, torn up, sliced up, or cut up scraps of paper in every color imaginable.

"Yeah. We refer to this room as 'tornado alley' and we call the trash 'design debris.' At some point, the floor becomes its own form of art," Gretchen chuckled.

As we were about to leave the studio, Bethany noticed a student splayed out on a raggedy and worn sofa in a far corner, dead-to-the-world asleep. When she stopped cold in her tracks to stare at him, we all did. "Are you allowed to sleep in class ... like *that?*" she almost demanded to know.

"Sure. As long as our projects are completed by the assigned deadlines," Gretchen matter-of-factly replied.

"Are you ... kidding me? We're not even allowed to put our heads on our desks. Oh ... my ... God," Bethany fumed as she shoved open the big double doors and stormed out of the room.

On our ride back to school, every kid on the bus swore an oath that they would all some day attend the College of Design.

MOMENTS AND MEMORIES

Most Embarrassing

I GOT TO SCHOOL VERY EARLY THAT MORNING. SO EARLY, IN fact, one of the custodians had not yet finished waxing and buffing B-Hall corridor floors. I needed to make enough copies of a multi-page handout for every student in each of my six classes to get one, that day, and I knew if I got behind a long queue of teachers at our one and only copier, I would not get that task done by the time homeroom started.

When I arrived at school, I headed straight to my class-room, grabbed the stack of material I needed to copy, and hustled off to the copier room. About halfway through the job, I decided to save some time by going to my mailbox-cubby to retrieve any internal mail I might have waiting there.

Leaving the copier chugging away, I rushed out of the room and down the hallway, knowing I had to hurry in case the copier jammed. Just after turning the corner onto the main corridor leading to the front office, totally oblivious to the yellow "CAUTION: Wet Floor" stanchion I passed, I strode full-speed onto a patch of liquid wax that was not yet dry. Before I realized what I had done or what was happening, both of my feet were straight out in front of me, about waist-high, and my butt was about to hit the floor, hard. When it did, I felt like I bounced at least three times, but I ignored the numbing pain and sprang back up like an embarrassed feline who had uncharacteristically fallen off the top of a fence. I was back on my feet so fast I was convinced you would need slow-motion video to even see me fall. Fortunately, I was not hurt, not even my pride, since there was no one present to witness my mishap.

On my way to the teachers' workroom at lunchtime that day, I encountered Mr. Callaghan in the hallway. "Mr. Massey, may I please see you in my office for a moment," he said.

Oh brother; now what?

As soon as we entered his office, he sat down at the keyboard of the security camera control system, executed a few keystrokes, turned the monitor towards me, and leaned back in the chair without saying a word. I looked at him, then at the monitor. There I was, in all my acrobatic glory ... both feet straight out ... my butt hitting the floor ... bouncing ... springing back up onto my feet ... looking around for witnesses. It was all playing back ... in sl-ow mo-ti-on.

"I'd score you a perfect ten on that maneuver," Mr. Callaghan chuckled.

Throughout the remainder of that week, he played that

video backwards, forwards, normal speed, fast-forward, slow motion, and freeze-frame, for every adult who came within shouting distance of his office. And he threatened to show it on our school-wide Channel 1 TV network during morning announcements.

Most Heartbreaking

ON A ROTATING BASIS, ALL TEACHERS AT OUR SCHOOL WERE expected to share in the responsibilities of conducting certain after-school activities, such as selling tickets to sporting events, or manning the concession stands. In most instances, however, unmarried teachers or older teachers with grown children volunteered so teachers with small children did not have to spend any more time away from home than academic obligations required of them.

"We need someone to help sell hot dogs at this afternoon's football game. If you can assist, please let Coach K (Kozak) know by lunchtime, so I don't have to draft someone," Mr. Callaghan might say during morning announcements, if push came to shove. But in this instance, I was drafted directly.

"The person scheduled to sell tickets at the basketball game today went home sick this morning; are you free to help me out?" Coach K, asked. In addition to coaching girls' basketball and volleyball, she was also our school's athletic director, and she knew I preferred helping out at basketball games because the ticket table was close enough to the action to also see the games.

On several occasions, I made a point of staying at school late, so

*I could go across the street and watch Isaiah Hicks play for our own
JF Webb High School Warriors before he moved on to Chapel Hill to
star for the University of North Carolina Tarheels.*

As soon as school let out that afternoon and the last of the
school busses departed—there are few things more liberating
for teachers than the sight of taillights on the ass-end of
school busses after having spent eight hours at a middle
school—I went to Coach K's office to fetch the money box,
which always contained a roll of *Admit One* tickets, $50 in
cash for making change, and a detailed reconciliation sheet to
be filed out accounting for each ticket sold, the $50 seed
money, and all ticket sales proceeds for that event, by individual coin and currency denominations. That was the part I
didn't like. If you were one cent off-tally, you would hear
about it, loud and clear, from Mrs. Fields, our bookkeeper.

Selling tickets to our school's sporting events always
presented me with a moral conundrum: Adults were charged
$4 for admittance—I had no problem with that—but all
middle-school- and high-school-aged kids had to pay $2 as
well. That was problematic. Some families could not afford
that; could not pay for their younger children to see their
older siblings play. So, I confess to cutting some kids a little
slack. (Sorry, Coach K. I know your program needed the
money, but you would have done the same thing.)

Our girls' basketball games started at four o'clock, but they
were sparsely attended, partly because a lot of parents had not
yet gotten off work, and partly because, even in middle
school, girls' basketball was not as popular as the boys' games,
which started about 5:30 p.m.

I was all set up, and just as the second game was about to

get underway, Brianna, one of my seventh-grade students, came over and sat down at the ticket table beside me.

"Can I help sell tickets?" she asked, smiling.

"I don't know; how high can you count; can you count to four?" I asked. Her smile broadened. "Okay," I said. "You take their money and put it in the box—remember to put twenties under the coin tray. I'll give them their change, then you give them their tickets, one for each paying person."

Between taking money, making change, issuing tickets, and watching the game, Brianna and I talked about school in general, but more so we talked about her day in particular, which according to her had not been half bad.

As soon as the second half of the boys' game began—that is when we were allowed to close-up shop—Brianna helped me count and reconcile the money box contents. I counted the number of individual $1, $5, $10, and $20 bills we had accumulated, and Brianna wrote each total on the accounting sheet. I recall we even had one $50 bill; an uncommon occurrence. After the bills, we did the same with half-dollars, quarters, dimes, nickels, and pennies. We didn't have many pennies. Whenever someone had to resort to pennies to buy a ticket, I usually let them slide. "Pay me next time," I would tell them. I also recall letting an elderly gentleman into a game once when he presented me with three $1 bills and a silver dollar to pay to watch his grandson play. "You'd better hang onto that thing, it looks like it might be real silver," I told him. "Much obliged," he said and stuffed the coin back into the pocket of his bib overalls.

With our reconciliation task completed, Brianna closed and latched the cash box as I removed two $1 bills from my pocket; the amount she had paid for her ticket. "Here you go; your wages for a job well done," I told her. She grinned and took it.

The next morning, as soon as first-period class started, Mr. Allen, one of our assistant principals, unlocked the door to my classroom, stepped inside, and motioned me out into the hallway.

"I'm going to keep an eye on your class for a few minutes. Mr. Callaghan wants to meet with all teachers in the counselor's conference area," he said, his face totally void of his usual characteristic grin.

Sure enough, when I got to the office, the entire faculty was assembled, and puzzled. Within minutes, Mr. Callaghan walked in, more pale and somber than I had ever seen him. He closed the door and got straight to the point.

"One of our students was killed in a car wreck, on the way to school earlier this morning," he said. All underlying murmuring instantly ceased and the room fell deafeningly silent.

"She was with her stepdad and sister, on Grassy Creek Road, when they hit a

patch of ice, skidded off the road, and hit a tree," he explained. I had never before seen him tear-up. The silence got more silent.

"Who was it?" Ms. Boyd haltingly asked, with dread in her voice.

"Brianna."

I am sure my instant intake of breath was audible. I immediately recalled her

wide-eyed smile a mere twelve hours earlier when I had

wished her a good night. "She never got to spend her two dollars," I thought. Then thought, "That's a strange thing for me to think about at this moment." Then it dawned on me. "Oh my God, I will still have Brianna's older sister Charley in my sixth-period class."

That day was by far the hardest of my teaching career, and one of the saddest of my life. That's when I realized that, with the exception of parents and grandparents, the sudden and tragic death of a child is perhaps hardest on their teachers.

Most Scary

ONE OF THE MOST WILLING AND HELPFUL STUDENTS I EVER taught was Rebecca. Through sheer initiative she practically made herself my class captain in sixth grade, and I made her class captain again in eighth grade simply because I missed her unbridled enthusiasm.

For a short while after she moved on to ninth grade, Rebecca would occasionally walk across the street from the high school after dismissal and help me make copies, wash and disinfect classroom tables, and sort supplies that had gotten scattered and scrambled. But those visits dwindled, and finally ceased, once Rebecca transitioned into the mindset of a high school student with high school interests and priorities.

One morning, about midway through the school year, Amanda—the same Amanda who was coming to my classroom during lunch periods on Tuesdays and Thursdays to read *Because of Winn Dixie* to me—stopped by my classroom as soon as her bus arrived at school. "Mr. Massey, Rebecca gave me this note to give to you," she said and handed me a sealed envelope.

"Gave it to you when?" I asked as I took the envelope and noticed my name scrawled on the front.

"Just now, when she got off the school bus at Webb High School. We ride the same bus," Amanda explained, and walked away.

I tore open the envelope. Rebecca had sealed and Scotch taped the flap shut.

Mr. Massey,
Will you please come over to my school today, maybe at lunchtime?
I need to talk to you. Things have gotten so bad at home I don't
know what to do anymore, but I have no one to talk to. I just want
to die. That will be better than this.
Rebecca

I immediately sought out Mr. Callaghan. He was out back in the parking lot

greeting the last of the arriving busses. I handed him the note. "I'd like to go over and talk to Rebecca at lunchtime," I requested.

"And say what to her? You're not trained to deal with situations like this; this is why we have guidance counselors." he replied. I said nothing. "Stay here and keep the busses from running over anyone. I'm going to take this note to Miss Barnett, tell her to call someone at Webb and tell them about this note, and ask that person to talk to Rebecca," Mr.

Callaghan told me. Before I could react or reply he was walking toward the building.

"But she's going to think I betrayed her confidence," I shouted out to him. He didn't respond.

At lunchtime, I went to see Miss Barnett, to check on Rebecca. Her door was closed, but I could hear the muffled sound of a young male voice. As I waited, it occurred to me how seemingly unusual it was for a male student to seek out the assistance of a guidance counselor.

"I called my counterpart at the high school earlier, but she was in a meeting. I left a message, asking that she call me back, but she hasn't. Not yet," Miss Barnett told me when I finally got in to see her.

"Did you tell her why you were calling?"

"No. I didn't want to record this kind of information on voicemail," she replied. "But I told her it was important," she added, sounding unduly nonchalant.

"I'd say this situation goes beyond *important*, and borders upon *life threatening*, wouldn't you?" I snapped in frustration and walked away.

As I walked back to my classroom—my fourth-period students would be arriving in five minutes—it occurred to me that Rebecca's lunch period had come and gone, that I had not shown up as she had asked, and that no one else had spoken with her about her anguish. "She probably thinks I got her note but ignored it." The thought of that possibility haunted me throughout the remaining three periods of the school day.

The dismissal bell rang at 3:15 p.m. By 3:20, I was in Miss Barnett's office. "I spoke with the counselor at Webb, she called Rebecca in, but Rebecca refused to talk to her; wouldn't tell her anything about what is going on."

"So, now what?"

"She'll try talking to her again tomorrow. But I remember Rebecca from when she was a student here, and as I recall, she was always a bit melodramatic."

"I hope we are all prepared to live with the consequences of this not being as simple as that." I was surprised by everyone's complacency.

The next morning, once again, Amanda showed up at my classroom door. "Mr. Massey, Rebecca asked when I gave you her note. I told her as soon as I got here, yesterday morning."

"When did she ask you that?"

"Yesterday afternoon, on the bus, on the way home."

"Did Rebecca say anything about it on the bus this morning?"

"I don't know. I didn't ride the bus. My mom brought me to school."

I immediately headed to the front office. "Good morning," Mrs. Love said when I walked up to the reception counter. I ignored her kind greeting.

"Will you please contact Mrs. Comer on her two-way and ask her to meet me at my classroom as soon as she can?" I requested, trying to sound urgent without sounding alarmed.

Mrs. Comer was one of our custodians, bus drivers, in-a-pinch substitute teachers, and mother of one of my students. She readily agreed to monitor my homeroom students and my first-period class, without asking questions.

"I have to run over to the high school, but I'll be back by second period," I promised, and hoped. "Please tell the kids in first period to complete the one-question quiz, then make sure their Walmart line graphs are up-to-date, then study for the upcoming Picasso quiz."

I doubted Mr. Callaghan would give me permission to leave our campus to go get involved in a situation like this at another school, but I assumed he would grant me forgiveness once he found out I had. But, to be on the safe side, I went out the back entrance of the gymnasium and walked around the building to the teachers' parking lot.

When I got to the high school I went directly to the principal's office and asked to speak with Rebecca, without getting into details. He buzzed the receptionist and asked her to check the attendance report and Rebecca's class schedule. "She's here, in world history class," he whispered to me, his hand over the mouthpiece. I breathed freely for the first time that morning. "Will you please page her to come to my office?" he asked the receptionist and hung up. "You can use my office," he said.

When Rebecca got to his office I could see she was relieved to see me. As soon as she walked in, the principal stood and walked out without saying anything other than, "Good morning," to her.

I opened our conversation with an apology for not coming to speak with her the day before, then said, "Rebecca, I am not qualified to help you when you get this distraught. But I care enough about your well-being to see that someone who is qualified to help you, does so. Okay?" She didn't respond. "*Okay?*" I asked again. Rebecca nodded as her eyes filled with tears.

Before I left to go conduct my second-period class at my

own school, I got Rebecca to agree that should she ever again feel like she might harm herself, she would seek support from her guidance counselor. "Or call Mrs. Love at our middle school and ask to speak to me. Or get off the bus at my school and come to my classroom. But no more notes, like this one; that's too iffy," I said. Rebecca said nothing. "Do you promise?" I asked. She shook her head without looking up from her fidgeting fingers. "Rebecca?" I said and paused until she looked at me. "Do ... you ... promise?"

"I promise," she whispered.

A male teacher hugging a female student was always fraught with risk. But so was not hugging them, appropriately, when circumstances dictated. I gave Rebecca a quick hug, and we both walked out of the principal's office and returned to our respective classes.

Rebecca somehow got involved in JROTC at her school and did very well, rising through the ranks to become a leader. Occasionally she would stop by my classroom after school, most often after she had done something noteworthy at school she wanted to share. A couple of times she was smartly attired in her JROTC Class A uniform, emblazoned with sergeant's stripes.

When I talked to Rebecca last, about a month before she graduated from high school, she told me she was planning to join the military. "I think the army. College isn't for me, Mr. Massey," she admitted, apologetically.

"College isn't right for a lot of people, and that's okay," I assured her.

Most Surprising

IT WAS AFTER 3:00 P.M. THE LAST PERIOD DISMISSAL BELL would be ringing soon. My eighth graders were packing up their belongings into their backpacks. I was roaming around, checking under tables and chairs for trash and trinkets to be picked up. As soon as I returned to my desk, there was a firm knock on my classroom door.

"Is that your scarf, on the bookshelf behind you?" I asked Denise, as I walked past, on my way to answer the door. Denise grabbed the scarf and stuffed it into her jacket pocket. "You're welcome," I said, politely, as a reminder that she had not been.

I opened the door, expecting to see a student from a previous class, asking if I had seen a wha-cha-ma-call-it or a thing-a-ma-jig they might have left behind earlier in the day. What I saw was a clean shaven young man with a fresh high-and-tight haircut, decked-out in his neat and pressed US Marine Corp dress uniform adorned with corporal's stripes. His cover—military jargon for hat—was tucked firmly under his left arm as he stood at ramrod-straight attention.

"Mr. Massey, do you remember me, Sir?" he immediately asked with an air of confidence. There was a familiarity about him, but it didn't rise to the level of recognition. "My name is Eric. I was in your art class about six years ago, except for all those days when you sent me to the office for acting a fool," he explained. "Or for being a knucklehead, as you put it," he said with a faint smile.

"Ah. Yes. Now I remember you, Eric," I replied. And I did.

Believe me. "But you looked different, somehow, back then," I said in jest.

"Yes, Sir. I was different back then. That's why I am here now. To apologize to you for the many times I disrespected you. And to thank you for not letting me get away with it, which would have been much easier to do, I am certain."

Eric's visit was brief—five minutes, max—and I have not seen nor heard from him since. But I still remember the expression of pride I saw on his face as he stood there in that hallway that day. A lot has happened in Iraq and Afghanistan since then. In light of that, I sometimes wonder and worry about Eric. As I recall, one of his least desirable qualities as a sixth grader was defiant unwillingness to back down from a fight or altercation—in the classroom, hallways, or cafeteria, or on the playground or school bus—the same quality that made him a good Marine, no doubt.

Most Gratifying

PERHAPS THE MOST UNFAIRLY FRUSTRATING ASPECT OF BEING A teacher is that in most instances, with most of our students, we never know if we succeeded or failed in our efforts to prepare them for a prosperous future and productive life. At heart, we know we both succeeded and failed, to varying degrees, with all students. On occasion, however, we encounter former students out in public who recognize and remember us, and expect us to recognize and remember them, even though they are bigger and more mature looking. That does not happen as often as I would like, but it does happen more than one might expect.

Hearing a cheerful "Hey Mr. Massey, remember me?" greeting from high-school-aged cashiers at Food Lions or the drive-through windows at McDonald's, or behind the counter at Ace Hardware stores or the hostess stand at restaurants, is always a pleasant but awkward experience as one must be careful how one responds to that question— "Remember me?" Most often, for some strange reason, it is former female students who ask. I always confidently reply, "Of course I remember you," and they usually follow-up with a dubious, "What's my name?" and a wry grin. "You're Beyoncé Knowles, right?" I always answer. They always smile ear to ear. At that point, I know I am in the clear.

My most recent former-student encounter happened at the Food Lion where Gerry and I frequently shop. When I arrived at the store, there was a huge fire truck in the parking lot, the engine idling. Inside the store I noticed two firemen with a cart full of groceries, mostly frozen pepperoni pizzas, Hot Pockets, Honey Nut Cheerios, and Pop Tarts.

When I got into the express checkout line with my package of still-warm chicken tenders and a family size bag of peanut M&Ms, the cashier in the regular line in front of me was almost finished ringing up the firemen. While one of the firemen continued working with the cashier, the other, a tall, lanky redhead, turned to me.

"Excuse me, Sir. What's your name?"

"Bill."

"I mean your last name."

"Massey."

"I thought so. My name is Greyson. You taught me in middle school. I was in your art class." He smiled and reached out to shake my hand. As soon as he told me his name, the image of the young man standing in front of me morphed in my memory to that scrawny little guy in sixth grade who never seemed to own a pencil or paper. "I've been a Raleigh fireman for almost four years," he proudly explained. I congratulated him on his career choice and thanked him for serving our community.

"It's my honor," he replied. I could tell he meant it.

When I finally got checked out—the elderly woman in front of me carefully scrutinized every item on her receipt before painstakingly paying the cashier in cash, including the use of dimes, nickels, and pennies—and got out to the parking lot, a third fireman who had waited outside was transferring bags of groceries from the shopping cart into the truck. Just as he was finishing, a young woman carrying a small boy walked up.

"Do you guys mind if my son looks inside the fire engine?" she asked.

One of the firemen reached out and the mother handed the boy to him. He turned and handed the child to Greyson, who was sitting in the truck's driver's seat. While Greyson pointed out various bells and whistles and shiny objects on the dashboard, the other fireman was fetching a small fireman's hat from somewhere inside the truck.

Greyson let the little boy toot the truck's air horn, then handed him back down to his mother. The other fireman placed the red plastic fireman's hat on the boy's head, and everyone departed, smiling.

Most Disheartening

OUR SCHOOL CONDUCTED UNANNOUNCED FIRE DRILLS FOUR times per school year. When the alarm bell sounded, all teachers and students filed out into the parking lot through pre-designated fire exit doors. Once there, teachers conducted headcounts while students milled around joking about how long they might be out of school if the building burned down. When the muffled all-clear bell was heard in the distance, everyone filed back into their classrooms in reverse order and whiled away the remainder of that now non- productive class period. From alarm bell to all clear, our fire drills lasted about fifteen to twenty minutes.

Twice a year, surprise tornado drills were also conducted whereby, when the principal announced, "TORNADO, TORNADO, TORNADO," over the PA system, all students were herded into the non-windowed, concrete block hallways right outside our classroom doors where they knelt side-by-side facing an interior wall, leaned forward placing their heads between their knees, covered their heads with their hands and arms, and remained crouched and quiet until the "All Clear" was announced. Tornado drills lasted less than ten minutes, during which quite a few embarrassed young ladies tried to compensate for wearing low-rise jeans by repeatedly reaching back and tugging down on the tails of their too-short shirts.

Fire and tornado drills were so commonplace that such emergency practice exercises had become ho-hum events.

Then came Newtown, Connecticut. Then came lockdown drills.

On December 14, 2012, twenty first and second graders were unthinkably shot and killed by a deranged gunman inside their classrooms at Sandy Hook Elementary School. So were five of their teachers and their principal.

About a quarter-way through the following school year, everyone at our school—teachers, staff, and students—underwent a lockdown procedures training session conducted by Officer C, our school's Resource Officer. Going classroom to classroom, he walked each teacher and all of his or her students through exactly where to hunker down inside their particular classroom, what to do, how to properly do it, and why.

"Under no circumstances do you unlock that door for *anyone*! Not for someone claiming to be a police officer. Not for your principal. Not even for me," Officer C emphasized. "Anyone with authorization to legitimately enter your classroom during or after a lockdown will have a master key, and will use it to open your door, when it is safe to do so." Even practicing for an active shooter event was frightful.

On a Monday morning in late November, right before Thanksgiving break, my second-period class of sixth-grade boys had finished their one-question quiz and we were about to begin reviewing for a quiz the next day on Claude Monet and Impressionism.

Suddenly, "LOCKDOWN! LOCKDOWN! LOCKDOWN!" blared from the PA speakers in our classroom. The kids instantly went fearfully wide-eyed. But, startled and alarmed though they were, they did exactly as they had been told. We turned off all lights, quickly gathered in the far corner of the classroom away from exterior windows and out of sight of the small window in our classroom door, and sat on the floor in a hushed huddle.

"Mr. Massey, is this a practice?" someone in the midst of the tightly bunched group whispered with a mixture of fear and hope in his voice.

"I don't know," I had to admit.

We remained that way for more than an hour, until there was a tap, tap, tap on our classroom door. "This is the police. Open up, please," a female voice softly said from the hallway. The kids looked at me. I put my finger to my lips making the "Shhh" signal. There were three more knocks. Louder. And the "Open up" request was repeated more forcefully. I shook my head "No," to the kids. Some of them shook their heads back.

About a minute later we heard keys rattling on the other side of the door, then heard the lock bolt turn. I am pretty sure all of us held our breaths for a brief moment until we saw a female police officer in uniform step into our classroom, followed by Officer C. The kids and I collectively, simultaneously exhaled.

The only thing I can think of that would make looking at fear that borders on terror in the eyes of your students more gut-wrenching for teachers would be the sound of gunshots ringing out from elsewhere in the building, and imagining the unimaginable.

38

A TIME TO SOW – A TIME TO STOP SOWING

I RETIRED FROM TEACHING THREE WEEKS SHY OF MY SEVENTY-second birthday. I was not burned out. I had not become disheartened. My enthusiasm had not diminished. But my eyesight had. As a consequence of glaucoma, my distance vision was closing in, so much so I had to give up driving, and I lived more than thirty miles from school.

Not many days go by without me missing my interactions with my students. They kept me sharp of mind, young at heart, and spry of step.

More so when I first started teaching, but occasionally still to this day, someone will ask me, "What was the biggest difference between working in corporate America, and teaching in middle school?"

"There are two differences," I explain. "One, my corporate customers never hugged me. And two, my middle school 'customers' were *supposed* to act like children."

39

SOME THINGS TEACHING TAUGHT ME

- As a teacher, if I wasn't getting better and better, from year to year to year, I wasn't doing my job.
- No matter how bad I thought *my* day was, there were at least a half-dozen kids sitting in front of me in every class who were having much worse days than mine, because their nights had been worse than mine, because their lives were worse than mine. And I needed to take that into account when setting day-to-day expectations of them— academically and behaviorally.
- Middle school kids will push you as far as you will let them, all the while hoping you will not allow them to push you too far.
- Kids who proclaim not to *like* you because you require them to behave themselves, almost always

respect you for it—especially those who protest loudest.

- Teachers can give kids proverbial kicks-in-the-butt when they deserve it, if they also give them a hug when they need it. Doing one is ineffective if you don't do the other.
- Even though they will never admit it, kids fear chaos and crave order and structure in their lives. For too many kids, school is the only place where stability is available to them.
- Kids will take an interest in whatever teachers make interesting. Turns out, Mark Twain was right when he said, "Teaching is twenty-five percent theory, and seventy-five percent theater."
- No, teachers should not try to *save them all*—only the ones sitting in front of them.
- I wish I had started teaching sooner. I wish I could have lasted longer.

40

FIRST AND FOREMOST

BEFORE ALL ELSE, KIDS *MUST* BE TAUGHT THREE THINGS: 1) HOW to read, and a love of reading—with reading proficiency will come a familiarity of grammar, punctuation, and spelling. 2) The fundamentals of math; the system—how it works, and why. 3) How to study; how to learn; the pride that comes with simply "knowing stuff"—the ability to learn anything.

41

IN A NUTSHELL

TEACHING DID NOT MAKE ME WEALTHY. IT ONLY MADE me happy.

ACKNOWLEDGMENTS

- To my wife Gerry, who supported my long days at school and short nights at home doing my "home work."

- To the more than 2,200 students who passed through my classroom; I learned something from each of you. Most prevalently, I learned that I had a lot to learn.

- To every parent who supported my efforts to educate their children and make them better people by holding them accountable to reasonable academic expectations and respectful behavior.

- To those who helped me become a teacher:

Dan Callaghan
Beth Cook
Sarah Renn

- To those who helped me become a better teacher:

Mike Allen
Karen Adcock Currin
Jackie Harris
Tonya Thomas

- To my colleagues who supported me while I was being a teacher:

Judy Elliott
Shirley Fields
Boyce Harvey
Terry Jennings
Robin Love

- To those who always answered my too-frequent pleas for outside assistance:

Susan Gilbert
Debra Morgan
Eric Tannery
Guy Tunstall
H.D. and Jan Cornelius

- To those who plied me with advice and expertise in the production of this book:

Al Carson
Josie Brown
Susan Gilbert

SPECIAL ACKNOWLEDGMENT

To Raz Autry, the only principle I can "remember" having during my twelve years as an always mischievous, most times rambunctious, sometimes misbehaving, oft-times under-achieving student at Gaston School. Mr. Autry paddled me once in fifth grade for jealously throwing a classmate's new Yankees baseball cap into a trash barrel fire at school, and he suspended me in ninth grade for leaving school grounds during lunch period without permission to buy hot dogs for my girlfriend and me from nearby Rook's Grill, but never told my daddy about either instance, because he knew my daddy would brutally react.

"One of these days, Boy, you're going to straighten up and fly right," he always said to me after one of my episodes of flying wrong. He was the first person I called to tell the day I received my teaching certificate in the mail. "Lord have mercy," he said, "There's hope for us all."

MY FAVORITE TEACHER

Throughout our lives, most of us are occasionally asked, "Who's your favorite teacher?" Nowadays, we are even asked that as a security question when setting up online or social media accounts. In my case—I don't fully know why—I always answer "Mister Willey."

Tom Willey was my high school shop teacher. He patiently taught us boys about, and how to use, hand tools, then took us to compete in tool identification contests at other schools in our county—Northampton. He also taught us to always observe safe practices when using power tools, then proceeded to cut off the index finger of his right hand on a DeWalt radial arm saw.

He never got (overly) angry, and he never "ratted us out," even when he caught us smoking.

Again, I can't quite put my finger (no pun intended) on

why Mister Willey has always been my favorite teacher; perhaps that is how it should be.

Made in the USA
Middletown, DE
25 August 2018